Get
Your Money
Right

Mary,

Keep making it
happen! And
transforming lives.

Get
Your Money
Right

The 7 Keys to Unlocking a Better Financial Future

KEMBALA EVANS

KP Evans Financial

Get Your Money Right
The 7 Keys to Unlocking a Better Financial Future

Copyright © 2011 by Kembala Evans

Published by KP Evans Financial.

KP Evans Financial
P.O. Box 59722
Schaumburg, IL 60159-0722
info@gainmoneycontrol.com; http://gainmoneycontrol.com

Scriptures included are taken from biblegateway.com.
Used by permission of Zondervan. www.zondervan.com.

Quotes unattributed are by Kembala Evans.

Cover photo © Feverpitched | Dreamstime.com.
Author Photo: Chicago Photographer Sri—www.PhotosBySri.com.
Book designed by Adina Cucicov at Flamingo Designs.

Library of Congress Control Number: 2011912107

ISBN 978-0-9835796-8-7

First Edition

DEDICATION

This book is dedicated in loving memory of Virginia Knighton (1951–2010), my aunt. Auntie Ginny was a special person who understood the meaning of love and walked in it everyday. Her strong encouragement and motivation helped me bring this book to completion. I'm truly thankful for having her in my life.

To my most important teacher, my mother, Susan Parkins. This work embodies many of the important life lessons you taught me, such as the importance of faith, wisdom, hard work, and love. Everything you instilled in me as a child has fueled my life's successes. I'm eternally grateful for you.

To my dear husband, Sam. You are the love of my life. Thanks for sharing your life with me and for believing in me. Your unconditional love and endless support helped shape me into the person I have become today! I am blessed to have a husband as special as you are in my life.

To my lovely daughters, Aaliyah and Kiara. You are my most precious blessings. Thank you for giving my life more meaning and inspiring me to be the best me I can be every day.

And to you (yes, you the reader!), this book also is dedicated. Thank you for investing the time in reading this book. It is my greatest hope that this book will make a positive impact on your life.

ACKNOWLEDGEMENTS

This book started with a vision for helping everyday people improve their personal finances. I thank God for giving me the vision, guidance, and fortitude to turn the idea (writing a book) into reality.

This would not have been possible without my clients, thank you for believing in me and for being open to using new techniques and strategies to reach your goals. It's been a privilege to work with you. Your success stories are my constant inspiration for helping others achieve their financial goals.

To my family, friends, mentors, and colleagues—I thank you for your encouragement, time, support and feedback.

I express my sincere gratitude to:
- My father, Bevin, for his constant guidance and for encouraging me to pursue my dreams.
- My sister, Anika, for her support, insightful thoughts and suggestions.
- My brother, Keino, for believing in me, listening, and offering his candid and thoughtful opinions.
- My grandmother, Gladys, for her inspiration and strong encouragement.
- My mother-in-law, Charlene, for her uplifting words of encouragement.
- My dearest friends Stephanie Williams and Lisa Bullard for their constant support, motivation, and friendship.

- My friend Mugosi Ombima, who spent many hours reviewing this book to provide thoughtful and useful feedback.

And for the development of the book itself, I thank:
- My former colleague Kim Le who strongly encouraged me to write this book. Thanks for giving me the extra push I needed to do what I knew needed to be done.
- Katina and Travis for your friendship. Also for allowing me to share our stories in this book.
- James Abdullah, Kerlin Blaise, Lanee Blaise, Alphonso Brown, Monty Cyriac, Jonathan Dixon III, Sharmion Ford, Valerie Henry, Kai Holmes, Anita Ibe, Christina Nicholas, Maurice Nicholas, Elba Pena, Jamillah Washington, and Marcus Williams for your valuable input, feedback, and support.
- TJ Butler, Fawn Germer, KA Murray, and Elveria Webb for taking the time to share your personal experiences, lessons learned, and words of wisdom as published authors.
- Dave Nelsen (www.thegrammargeek.com), my editor, who transformed my manuscript into a book.
- Adina Cucicov, my talented book designer, for bringing my vision to life and making it even better.

There are many others who have contributed to this book with their thoughts, ideas, and suggestions. While you may not be named individually, I sincerely thank you for your contributions.

SUMMARY OF CONTENTS

Introduction 1

Key #1: Develop the Right Mindset 17

Key #2: Establish Your Vision and Goals 33

Key #3: Watch Where Your Money Goes . . . Literally! 51

Key #4: Live Below Your Means to Get Ahead 83

Key #5: Drop the Debt Weight 113

Key #6: Save in More Ways than One 137

Key #7: Be Grateful and Give Freely 179

Ready to Take Action? 193

About the Author 197

What is Junior Achievement? 199

TABLE OF CONTENTS

Introduction 1
  My Turning Point 2
  Our Society Today 4
  Money Management: Just Common Sense? 6
  How I Learned About Money 9
  Why You Need to Keep Reading 13

Key #1: Develop the Right Mindset 17
  Look Forward 18
  Think Positive! 20
  Do You Have an Attitude? 23
  Power of Words 26

Key #2: Establish Your Vision and Goals 33
  Create Your Vision 33
  Set Your Goals 37

Key #3: Watch Where Your Money Goes . . . Literally! ... 51
  Where to Start Watching 56
  Bank Smart 60
  Be Credit Wise 67
  Home Equity, Mortgage, and Other Loans 71
  Student Loans 72
  Utilities, Cable, Internet, and Other Services 74
  Medical Bills 75
  Watch the Cash Register 75

Invest Wisely 76
Track Your Money 79
Get Started 80

Key #4: Live Below Your Means to Get Ahead 83
Do You Have a Budget? 86
Why Are People Living Above Their Means? 92
How to Avoid the Debt Trap 96
Breaking Away From the "Now" Society 100
Standing Your Ground, Despite the Pressure 101
Divas Live Below Their Means Too 104
Live Your Life and Forget About the Joneses 105
Improve Your Financial Understanding 106
Be a Disciplined Spender 108

Key #5: Drop the Debt Weight 113
Three Big Reasons to Drop the Debt Weight 116
Your Credit Matters 116
Debt Impacts Relationships 122
Quality of Life 126
It's Time to Drop the Debt Weight 127
Are You Thinking About Settling Your Debt? 134

Key #6: Save in More Ways than One 137
Establish Your Personal Savings Emergency Fund 140
Save for the Future 142
Why Save for Retirement? 143
Retirement Savings Plans 145
Individual Retirement Accounts 151
Retirement Saver's Credit 154
Saving for College 154
Large Purchases 156

Shop Smarter..157
Save on Services..170

Key #7: Be Grateful and Give Freely..............179
Be Grateful for What You Have...............................180
Give Freely...184
Why Give?...186

Ready to Take Action?...193

About the Author...197

What is Junior Achievement?.............................199

INTRODUCTION

*If you can perceive it, just believe it,
and you will achieve it.*

At the time of this writing, we are in the midst of a big re-cession. This recession has been so devastating that it's been called an "economic crisis" and "The Great Recession." Hearing about company layoffs, home foreclosures, and financial institutions failing has become the norm from today's news media. And it is the uncertainty of what tomorrow may bring that compelled me to write this book.

Despite this bleak economic climate, I created my own defining moment when I decided to leave my company. After dedicating nearly twelve years of service to one of the world's leading global consulting companies, Accenture, I left. Many of my colleagues and clients were shocked to hear about my career decision, especially given that I was a senior manager and had been with the company for so long.

After all, I enjoyed being a consultant and helping our *Fortune* 500 clients improve their businesses. In fact, I had always dreamed of making partner and was only one step away from it. The decision to leave was a tough one, and it appeared as though I was giving up everything I had worked so hard to accomplish in my career.

Nonetheless, I could not shrug off my strong desire to become more of a blessing to others.

You may be asking why I resigned despite the economic climate. What could I possibly do to become more of a blessing to others?

These are valid questions, and I will do my best to answer them.

You see, at the time, I'd already spent more than a decade coaching family, friends, colleagues, and absolute strangers in personal finance, and it was a privilege to help people change their money habits and reach their financial goals.

I'm very passionate about helping people achieve goals they never dreamed possible. From the person who was too embarrassed about his poor credit rating of 532 to the young lady who never thought she would be able to save money—it is very fulfilling to help them succeed and reach their financial goals (improve credit, eliminate debt, build savings).

My Turning Point

Now, to answer those two questions more directly, I'd like to share my personal turning point. One morning while preparing for work, I started questioning and pondering what my real purpose was in life. And for some reason, I just had this strong feeling that it was different from what I had been doing professionally as a consultant. So I knew my current career path would not get me there.

Later that morning, on my way to work on the train, something unexpected happened. I heard a woman's voice call out to me. She said, "Hey, you look like you would know the answer to this question. Will unpaid medical bills mess up your credit?" This woman had never spoken to me before in my life. I asked her if she was talking to me, and she immediately nodded her head.

Then, I happily answered her question. I don't recall specifically what I said, but I do remember how my answer spawned a lively discussion on a variety of personal finance topics. Our conversation easily captivated other train passengers, who started chiming in with their own thoughts and questions.

We talked about mortgages, people living paycheck to paycheck (literally a paycheck away from poverty), and living above your means. I was so intrigued with the conversation that I didn't even notice our talk had lasted the entire commute into downtown Chicago, which was about forty-five minutes.

This energetic discussion proved to me that there is a considerable need to share personal finance knowledge in a simpler way. It also confirmed what I had always thought was my purpose in life—teaching people about personal finance in an easier and more meaningful way. It was an amazing conversation, and it felt as though feelings of hopelessness were transformed into those of hope, which is a good thing.

This personal experience seemed to answer the question of what my purpose is in life. Being able to share my knowledge and experience on the subject and listen to their personal stories just made me feel like I was in the right place. And this sentiment seemed to have been mutual, because I overheard people asking about me and making positive comments about the discussion as I exited the train.

I will remember that day for the rest of my life, because it ignited in me the desire to expand my reach in helping more people improve their personal finance knowledge so they can live better. I enjoy making a positive difference in the lives of those around me.

With that said, choosing to leave a company where you have been highly productive for nearly twelve years and are literally one promotion away from partner, during a time of economic uncertainty, was still very challenging. Fortunately, I was in the financial position to be able to leave and pursue my dreams. But I must admit walking away from a promising career and a comfortable six-figure income took a lot of courage to do. I know there are few willing to take on the risk needed to pursue their dreams, ambitions, and personal aspirations. However, my strong faith and burning desire to help everyday people allowed me to make this seemingly difficult decision an easy one. Yes, this is my response to those questions. That's why I resigned, and that's what I thought I could do to become a blessing to others.

Our Society Today

Our economic climate, which, sadly, is filled with home foreclosures, failing financial institutions, and many questionable spending decisions at all levels (e.g., personal, government) begs for people to become more financially literate and responsible. Although many books have been written on the topic of money, my goal is to focus on the core principles of personal finance that will have the greatest impact on your life today. This book simplifies important financial concepts, provides an interactive experience, and gives you practical tips you can use to create a better financial future.

The need to increase our financial understanding and change the behaviors that got many of us to where we are today is glaring. It is evident that we have spent the last few decades becoming a "now" society. A now society is one that seeks instant gratification and creates a strong desire to make purchases *today*. There has been a shift away from saving and toward spending. And in many cases, we're spending more than we make. After all, we have been provided easy access to credit, which gives us more purchasing power.

For many of us, having the credit available creates an urge to buy it and have it now, then just pay for it later. Even if the urge is not there, we hear the messages over and over in commercials, mail solicitations, and credit offers encouraging us to "buy now, pay later."

And there is less of an emphasis being put on verifying whether it is something we *need* or something we should choose to *save for now* and *buy later*. It's time that we get back to the basics, and this book lays the foundation for that change to occur.

It includes many of the techniques I have used to help people improve their money management skills and achieve their personal financial goals. My mother always said, "If you keep doing the same thing, you'll get the same results." This book was written to inspire you to change what you're doing to get better results.

> *"Insanity: doing the same thing over and over again and expecting different results."*
> **–Albert Einstein**

Real change comes from the inside out. And YOU must be willing to drive the change you desire to achieve success. Reading this book is a step in the right direction. It is my hope that you will find this book instrumental in helping you transform your life.

> *"Accept responsibility for your life. Know that it is you who will get you where you want to go, no one else."*
> **–Les Brown**

Money Management: Just Common Sense?

Although many people were excited about my decision to pursue my dream, one friend's response surprised me. It was unforgettable and quite astonishing, to say the least.

I had lunch with a friend, Travis, and the main topic of discussion was my new venture. I started the conversation with a lot of energy, explaining how passionate I was to help people improve their understanding of personal finance so they could live better. I told him how rewarding it was to coach people to achieve financial goals they never thought possible. And I stressed that, given our current economic climate, it was more urgent than ever to help people improve their money management skills.

Travis responded very bluntly, "That's common sense. Everyone should know how to handle money."

I was surprised by his condescending remark. Just common sense? I instantly replied that it was not simply common sense, especially given that the subject (money management) is rarely taught in schools. Then he took a moment to think about my response. There was a bit of silence, until I asked him how he learned about money and handling his personal finance matters.

Travis then exclaimed with a puzzled look, "Well, my dad is really good at handling money and he taught me all about it! He really drilled the principles into us as kids."

I began to smile, because his response was fully in line with what I expected. I welcomed the opportunity to discuss how people learned about money with him. Then I said, "Yes, you learned from your father, and he must have taught you good money habits."

He nodded his head in agreement. Then I said, "Well, everyone is not as fortunate as you were to have that type of personal finance teaching."

We were finally in complete agreement, as he replied with a smile, "Yeah, you're right."

It's funny how some people may not see the need for something when it's not their own.

This conversation confirmed my initial thoughts on how people learn to handle their money. Personal finance was not something everyone learned in school. Unfortunately, it didn't make the required subject matter list, like math or science. However, it's a subject that greatly impacts us, including our relationships and our quality of life. Given this significance, I find it disturbing that it's something we often must pick up in our surroundings and are not formally taught.

Our personal finance teachers come from different backgrounds and are more likely to be those around us, such as family members, caretakers, friends, and mentors. Therefore, the quality of such random education is inconsistent. Robert Kiyosaki described the way we learn about money in his book *Rich Dad, Poor Dad*:

> *One of the reasons the rich get richer, the poor get poorer, and the middle class struggles in debt is because the subject of money is taught at home, not in school. Most of us learn about money from our parents. So what can a poor parent tell their child about money? They simply say "Stay in school and study hard." The child may graduate with excellent grades but with*

*a poor person's financial programming and mind-set. It was
learned while the child was young.*[1]

I agree with Kiyosaki's perspective; the personal finance teaching we receive can strongly influence the way we handle our money.
Unfortunately, the problem lies in the fact that there are far more
people who teach poor money management skills. On the other
hand, some of us who may have observed poor money management
behavior strive to learn good money management skills from someone else. This could be compared to someone who grew up with a
parent who was an alcoholic. Although she is exposed to alcoholism,
she makes up her mind not to follow in the same footsteps and completely avoids repeating the same behavior later in life.

If you're struggling to manage your money today or were taught
poor money management skills, this book is for you. This book
reveals the secret personal finance principles to help you manage
money effectively, make more informed financial decisions, and improve your quality of life—so you can break the cycle and teach others good money management skills.

---

1   Robert T. Kiyosaki with Sharon Lechter, *Rich Dad Poor Dad: What the Rich
Teach Their Kids About Money That the Poor and Middle Class Do Not* (New
York: Business Plus, 2010), 14.

How I Learned About Money

My mother initially taught me about money, and her method of teaching did not follow any Money 101 format. I learned through observation: the words she spoke, the actions she took, and the interactions she had with others regarding money. My learning environment may not have been the most ideal, but it was real.

My mother was one of eight children growing up in a very rural part of North Florida. She was a very bright student who graduated from college with excellent grades. Eventually, my mother met my father, got married, and started a family. Both of my parents strived to raise their children in a safe environment with access to good education. As a result of their efforts, we lived in a nice neighborhood in a suburb of Jacksonville, FL. I started learning about money around the age of six. Most of my learning happened during shopping trips or credit union visits with my mom. As an inquisitive child, I asked her many questions about money: Where does money come from? What is a check? Why do you go to the credit union? My mother taught me where money came from and how it was used to pay for goods and services.

Several years later, my life drastically changed—with my parents' divorce. In fact, it was the most significant experience of my childhood. Because my parents' divorce significantly changed our quality of life as a family, the lessons I learned about money became more impactful.

When my mother unexpectedly became a single parent, bearing most of the responsibility of raising three young children, we moved from our single-family home in the suburbs to a more affordable townhouse in Jacksonville. This is when I really began to understand the impact money had on our lives. My brother and I were in fourth and fifth grade, respectively, and my baby sister was only two years old at the time. We seemed to have gone quickly from a carefree way of living, in which my father primarily handled the finances, to one in which my mother mastered the art of stretching every dollar and prioritizing expenses.

My mom worked very hard to provide for us. Based on the conversations I overheard growing up, my father did not seem to be helping out much financially, which largely contributed to the burden my mother carried as a single parent. My mother had the heavy responsibility of raising three young children on her own, with credit card bills on top of it. This must have been a lot for my mom to deal with personally, but she's such a resilient and strong woman that we never saw it. She always said, "God doesn't give you more than you can handle," and she proved that to be true every day.

My mom worked a full-time job that provided a rewarding career. And she wanted to continue to raise us in the same manner as she did before her divorce, placing a high priority on the type of neighborhood we lived in, with access to great schools. After a few short years we moved back to the suburbs and into a four-bedroom single-family home. Although we made the move, she was still not receiving enough money from my dad to support our family. As a result, we started "living above our means," and that comes with many challenges.

You are living above your means when your monthly expenses exceed your monthly income. I'm sure it would have been different had my father been contributing more support. But to make up the income difference my mother decided to take on part-time jobs and use her sewing talents. Despite the circumstances and challenges, my mom's strong faith and dedication helped her overcome it all.

The life lesson she taught me along the way was the power of faith. And there were many money lessons too.

As a child I tried to look for ways to help her minimize expenses. Who would have thought I'd later become a financial coach? I remember one day when I overheard my mom talking on the phone about all the bills that she had to pay and how she didn't have enough money. I quickly thought about the free lunch program at school and told her that it might be an option for her to save money on our lunch. The next day at school I asked for the form to fill out to see if my mother would qualify for the program. I turned it in—only to be told that we did not qualify. The school administrator responded pleasantly with a smile as she handed the form back, saying, "You can come back when your mom makes a lot less money."

I couldn't believe it, because, judging by the way my mom spoke about money, I thought we would definitely qualify. However, I later came to realize that my mother's income was considered middle class, and only lower-income households qualified for the program. This news really surprised me. Her single salary was more than some families' combined household income, but she still struggled to stay on top of all the bills as a single parent. This showed me the importance of making sure your expenses are reasonable compared to your income, regardless of how much money you make. Because when your expenses exceed your income, it adds a tremendous amount of stress and pressure to your life.

We must always remember children are very impressionable and tend to learn more from our actions than by what we say. During the many years I spent watching my mother raise us, some valuable money lessons I learned were:

- **How we talk about money influences our reality.**
  The way my mother spoke or felt about money closely aligned with what manifested in her life. She used to say, "I don't have any money." And despite her income, there were times when she struggled to pay the bills and make ends meet. She would also say, "I can't afford it." We would hear this response to anything that was not deemed a necessity. It was like magic; she would say she couldn't afford it, and that always seemed to hold true.

- **Prioritize your money.**
  One day, when my mother and I were talking about this book, I asked her what the most important money lesson was that she taught me. She immediately responded, "Prioritization." I assured her it was already in the book. After all, my mother's greatest strength was how she prioritized her expenses. And she's right: it's very important to distinguish between wants and needs. She always prioritized our living expenses (rent, utilities) and necessities above anything else she may have wanted, such as a new outfit. And I'm happy to say that, because she did this so well, we always had everything we needed growing up. Thanks mom!

- **Money may affect how we feel and look.**
  Our feelings about money or a specific financial situation can impact our well-being. My mother appeared emotionally drained during the most difficult times she had managing her finances. Financial stress can impact our lives in many ways. For example, a friend told me about a sharp pain she was having in her arm. When she described the severity of the pain, I felt inclined to ask about her finances. After talking about her financial *problems*, it was quite clear to both of us that the pain was really due to her financial *stress*.

In summary, my mother taught me about money through her actions, words, and emotions. Overall, I was able to learn many important lessons in money management, and this learning laid the foundation for my financial understanding. Sure, there may have been a few times when she demonstrated poor money management, but they were actions she deemed necessary to make it through as a single parent raising three young children. And these few instances taught me about the extra costs and ramifications that come with certain financial decisions.

To improve my financial knowledge and money management skills, I looked for mentors to teach me. For example, my uncle, who my mother would often say had "A-1 credit" (meaning good credit), shared his financial wisdom with me. I also gained knowledge by reading countless financial books and magazines. After college, I worked as a personal banking specialist, which helped me build additional financial knowledge. Now, I would like to "pay it forward" and share my knowledge and experience with you.

Why You Need to Keep Reading

Imagine how different your life would be if you had more control of your money. More importantly, how would you feel?

Well, this book reveals the important financial principles to help you get your money right, so you can:
- Stop stressing and start living,
- Spend less and save more,
- Manage your money better,
- Improve your credit score, eliminate debt and
- Enjoy life!

If you're tired of doing the same old thing and getting the same results, then *Get Your Money Right* is the book for you. This book will show you how to use proven strategies to help you improve your finances. It includes real-life success stories (however, in most cases the actual names and identifiable details have been changed to protect my clients' identities) and is packed with practical money-saving tips that you can put into action now. It also reveals many of the financial principles that the rich use to stay rich.

Unlike some financial books, this book makes learning about money easy. My vision was to create a personal finance book that would be easy to understand and simple to use.

Get Your Money Right focuses on the core principles of personal finance to help you create a better financial future. I have divided it into seven keys focused on the most important financial principles and each key breaks down the personal finance concept in an easy-to-understand and to-the-point fashion.

This book will show you how to change what you're doing to get better results.

You Can Change Your Money Habits

On a trip to the store, I noticed two people ahead of me in line who tried to pay for their purchases on credit cards. The scene was not a pleasant one to watch, as both of their credit cards were denied. They weren't surprised by the denial and just reached for other cards to cover their purchases. Again, both cards were denied. Then, one customer shook her head in disbelief and paid cash. The other reached for another credit card that was finally approved.

I don't know their personal stories, other than what I observed that day. It saddens me to see people who are struggling with their finances. They probably feel like there is no way out. It is my hope that this book will provide you with the knowledge to break that cycle and create new habits for a healthier financial life. This is the real fuel behind this book, as it will provide you with the financial knowledge and inspiration to change your behavior, which in turn will positively impact your financial future.

The Solution
Knowledge paired with action is the solution. This experience can be compared to a traveler who has been walking through a treacherous and dark tunnel to reach a destination. The journey has been tiresome and difficult to navigate in the dark. However, suddenly, off in the distance, a light (knowledge) appears. This light provides the traveler with an easier path to follow. The traveler is now able to use the light to guide him or her to make the right steps and reach the destination much sooner.

Understanding personal finance gives you the knowledge to make more informed financial decisions and to avoid overpaying for products and services. Most importantly, you can take control of your financial future, so you have more peace of mind and security. This book is aimed at helping you get your money right. However, knowledge alone will not get you there; you must be willing to take action to achieve success. The value of this knowledge, paired with your commitment to take action, is priceless. Believe me, I have seen it firsthand in the people's lives that I have been fortunate to touch.

Having good money management skills will help you improve your quality of life. Sleepless nights, fears, and stress due to financial concerns will start to go away as you build knowledge and take action to drive positive changes in your life. Your confidence in your ability to manage money will instill in you a sense of financial harmony.

Poor money management is one of the leading contributors to divorce, so this could even help your marriage or relationships. The best part is, it will help your family. Remember, children learn more from our actions than our words. Through your actions, you can help your children develop good money management skills, which will pay off for generations to come.

Thank you for reading this book! I wish you all the best in gaining the knowledge you need to improve your personal finances and quality of life.

Key #1

DEVELOP THE RIGHT MINDSET

"The most expensive piece of real estate is the six inches, give or take an inch or two, between your right ear and left ear. It's what you create in that area that determines your wealth. We are only limited by our minds."
–Dolf de Roos, www.dolfderoos.com

If you want to *Get Your Money Right*, then you have to start by getting your mind right—it all starts and stems from your mind. You have to start with your mindset to drive real change in your life. In other words, you may need to change your mindset to get what you truly desire.

After all, everything starts inside your mind. When you woke up this morning, it was because something in your mind told you to get up—even if you may have heard that annoying alarm clock going off, because you could have easily pressed snooze all day. All of your actions are powered by your thoughts. You have acted on your thoughts throughout your day, even in reading this book. Right?

According to the Merriam-Webster online dictionary, "mindset" is formally defined as:
    1: a mental attitude or inclination
    2: a fixed state of mind[2]

Your mindset is the internal drive that you will need to affect the life you live today. It is essentially something that starts from within and then branches out externally to what will become your future. The key components of your mindset are thoughts, attitude, and words. It may take some changes on your part to think and speak differently, but it will make all the difference in your being able to *Get Your Money Right*!

> *"The significant problems we have cannot be solved at the same level of thinking with which we created them."*
> **–Albert Einstein**

Look Forward

> *Letting go of what happened in the past makes it easier to press forward today.*

The best way to move forward is to start looking in that direction. Sure, we must learn from our past mistakes, but we have to let go in order to keep moving. In other words, stop focusing on past mistakes and start making the changes necessary to get back on track.

---

2   By permission. From *Merriam-Webster's Collegiate Dictionary*, eleventh ed. (Merriam-Webster, Inc., 2010), www.Merriam-Webster.com.

One morning I was watching Pastor Joel Osteen deliver a sermon on TV, and he used an analogy referencing the purpose of a rearview mirror and the windshield in a car. Pastor Osteen stressed the point of looking forward at where you are headed instead of looking back at where you've been. He said the reason the windshield is bigger than the rearview mirror is because it is more important to see where you are headed than where you were.

This analogy is a good one. Although it is important to reflect back on past mistakes, we must not dwell on them so much that we lose sight of our true destination. This reasoning holds true for your finances, too, because it's not about playing the blame game or beating yourself up about what you did wrong in the past. It is about making the commitment to change what you're doing to get better results.

It's all about you, because you are in complete control of your destiny. After all, you're in the driver's seat, and you can achieve whatever you want in life.

I commend you for reading this book and taking a step forward in the right direction! Gaining knowledge and using new techniques will help you transform your behavior and ultimately reach your financial goals in life.

Think Positive!

> *"The positive thinker sees the invisible, feels the intangible,*
> *and achieves the impossible."*
> **–Unknown**

The children's book *The Little Engine That Could* tells a powerful story about how what you think can make all the difference. The story is about a little train engine that had a difficult task before him in reaching his target destination. His determination throughout the challenging journey illustrates the power of being optimistic and working hard to achieve your goal.

The most important part of the story was the strong belief the engine carried with him to make it across the tough terrain and complete his journey. He would puff along and say "I think I can, I think I can, I think I can." These words became the most famous and memorable from the story. He thought he could do it, despite how challenging it appeared. In the end, it was the fact that he thought he could do it that led him to a successful journey.

This may have been a children's story, but I believe the concept of positive thinking holds true in adult life. Whatever you think and say every day has the power to influence the outcomes in your life.

How would you describe your mindset today? Is there anything you need to change about it? It all starts inside you, and your mind is very powerful. Do you think your thoughts have limited you in life?

There is power in your thoughts. The way you think has the ability to impact your reality. Some people believe in the law of attraction. Rhonda Byrne's book *The Secret* describes the law of attraction:

The law of attraction is a law of nature. It is impersonal and it does not see good things or bad things. It is receiving your thoughts and reflecting back to you those thoughts as your life experience. The law of attraction simply gives you whatever it is you are thinking about.[3]

Whether or not you believe in the law of attraction, there is a great amount of evidence to support that your thoughts do have the ability to influence things in life. There have been many studies to support this. For example, positive thinking has been known to help those who are facing terminal illnesses feel better.

Let's choose to think positive! If you think positive, you will become more optimistic and are bound to have better results. The way we think turns into words, and the words we speak can turn into action. If you start by thinking positively, then you will have more positive experiences.

When you think of money, what thoughts come to your mind? If any of those thoughts are limiting or negative, then develop the right mindset, one that thrives on positive thoughts. If you start thinking differently, change is soon to follow. The power of your new way of thinking will start a chain reaction and propel you in a more favorable direction.

You have the ability to change the way you think because you are in control. I can think of so many examples in my life when I looked beyond today for something better tomorrow. I thought it, I said it, and it happened. It really came to pass in that order, too. I also had faith and truly believed it. The timing is the only thing that varied.

---

3   Rhonda Byrne, *The Secret* (New York: Atria Books, 2006), 13.

One of my favorite verses from scripture is Mark 11:24:

"Therefore I say unto you, What things soever ye desire, when ye pray, believe that ye receive them, and ye shall have them."
–Mark 11:24 (King James Version)

This scripture means a lot to me, so much that if you were to look in my high school senior yearbook you would see it printed under my picture.

When it comes to your mindset, the power of your thoughts, faith, and what you truly believe combined are what makes things happen. So take a moment to reflect back on your thoughts. Ask the following questions:

- Are you dwelling on the past?
- Are you limited by the way you think?
- Do you think positive today? If not, what can you do differently to become more positive?

After you do this, start making any necessary changes to get the results you desire in life. Like many things, it will take practice. There may be times when you have to catch yourself, but being cognizant of this really helps you become more aware of what you are thinking and become more positive. After all, what could you lose by doing it? If it works, you have gained quite a bit.

"For as he thinketh in his heart, so is he"
–Proverbs 23:7 (King James Version)

Do You Have an Attitude?

"Attitude is a little thing that makes a big difference."
–Winston Churchill

Everyone has one, right? It's funny how there is such a negative connotation associated with the word "attitude." The word is oftentimes used to describe someone who is demonstrating poor behavior. However, everyone possesses an attitude about something. This attitude may be positive or negative, but everyone has one.

What is your attitude toward life and your finances? How would the people around you describe your attitude? If you don't know, ask. Many times those around us can provide an honest perspective on this, which can be very useful in driving change.

Your attitude is simply an expression of your innermost feelings. It starts inside with your thoughts (your mindset) and is unveiled through your expressions. Attitude is an important component of your mindset, so if it's negative, then it contradicts what you are trying to accomplish.

"What lies behind us and what lies before us are tiny matters compared to what lies within us."
–Ralph Waldo Emerson

Take a moment and think about your attitude toward your finances and life. Here are some questions you may want to consider:
- Do you have a "can do" attitude?
- Do you always dwell on what you can't do and why?
- Are you always talking negatively or being pessimistic about your finances?

23

- How would someone describe your attitude toward life?
- Do you view yourself as an optimist or a pessimist? Why?

When it comes to money, are you showing a rich or poor mentality? A rich mentality is one that sees no limits, seeks opportunities, and is full of determination to reach beyond the present circumstances for what it envisions to have in the future. A poor mentality focuses on the obstacles and finds it difficult to look beyond the present circumstances.

Your attitude has a lot to do with where you are today. If you think of all the reasons you can't do something, then you simply won't, because you have already limited yourself by your thoughts.

"If you think you can, you can.
And if you think you can't, you're right."
–Mary Kay Ash

Yes, there is power in your thoughts. I'd like to share a poem by Walter D. Wintle that shows you just how much what you think matters. This poem was written in the early 1900s and has been titled "Thinking" and "The Man Who Thinks He Can."

If you think you are beaten, you are
If you think you dare not, you don't.
If you like to win, but you think you can't
It is almost certain you won't.

If you think you'll lose, you're lost
For out of the world we find,
Success begins with a fellow's will
It's all in the state of mind.

If you think you are outclassed, you are
You've got to think high to rise
You've got to be sure of yourself before
You can ever win a prize.

Life's battles don't always go
To the stronger or faster man
But soon or late the man who wins
Is the man WHO THINKS HE CAN![4]

The message is straightforward and easy to understand. And there is overwhelming truth in the words. The strong message it sends to the reader is that what happens in your life starts and ends with what you think. That's why the first key is to **Develop the Right Mindset**. And it's best to have a "can do" attitude.

Would you consider yourself someone with a "can do" attitude? Your attitude reflects your innermost thoughts, and it has the power to enable you to accomplish great things. Someone with a "can do" attitude in life is bound for success.

Another inspiring poem worth reading is "Equipment" by Edgar A. Guest. I encourage you to search for a copy on the Internet. In his poem, he makes it clear that if someone else can do it, then so can you! You have everything you need to get anything done and succeed; all you need is confidence, which starts with the two simple words "I can." This inner confidence becomes your attitude about life, and in it is your ability to succeed.

---

4   Walter D. Wintle, accessed April 17, 2011,
    http://oldpoetry.com/opoem/119016-Walter-D-Wintle-Thinking.

I have a saying that I often use in life (look familiar?): **"If you can perceive it, just believe it, and you will achieve it."**

Remember YOU control your own destiny. If you can envision something, believe it without any doubts or fears, and have the courage to do it, then you are bound to accomplish whatever it is you set out to do. Your attitude is instrumental in making this happen, though. So reflect on where you are today and implement any necessary changes to improve your attitude on life.

You have to drive the change you seek from the inside out, and your attitude is an important component in developing the right mindset to get you there. If you need to improve your attitude, take steps to develop a positive "can do" attitude.

> *"The greatest discovery of my generation is that a human being can alter his life by altering his attitudes."*
> —William James

Power of Words

> *"Handle them carefully,*
> *for words have more power than atom bombs."*
> —Pearl Strachan Hurd

The words we speak are extremely powerful. We have the freedom to choose the words we speak, and they can be cynical, hopeful, positive, or negative. The choice is ours to make, but we must always remember there is power in the words we speak every day.

I have seen the impact words have made on my life and the lives of others. Have you? Think about it: have you ever heard someone say something that seemed farfetched? However, the person kept repeating it over and over. Then, it finally happens. How about in your life? Have you said something and then seen it manifest in your life?

As I noted in the introduction of this book, the words we use have the ability to influence our reality. This holds true for money management as well as in other areas of our lives. So, it is important that we pay closer attention to the words we use to create more desirable outcomes. After all, the words we choose have the power to impact our lives and the lives of others. They may inspire people to know they can accomplish great things or negatively impact their views of themselves.

I once heard about a study that proved how words could directly affect performance. It was conducted at a school, where a class was divided into two distinct sections. One section was made up of students who did well in school, and the other comprised low-performing students. The intent of the study was to understand whether the way the students were treated and spoken to would impact their performance and the way they viewed themselves. During the study, the lower performing students were praised and told they were bright students, while those who had previously been regarded as the high performers in the class were told they did not do good work. The results were amazing, as the students who had poor grades prior to the study saw their performance and confidence improve. Conversely, the work and attitudes of the students who had been high performers deteriorated. This study clearly illustrated how words could influence behavior, attitudes, and work ethic.

Another example that shows the impact words can have on someone's life happened to me in college, when I volunteered with a friend to spend some time with a local Girl Scout troop. The troop was located in Richmond Heights, FL, a suburb located about thirty minutes south of Miami. The girls were so excited to see me and could not believe that I went to the University of Miami. As I got to know them better, I started to ask them about their goals in life. I asked one girl, who was about ten years old, what college she wanted to attend. And her response is one that I will never forget.

She looked up at me with her bright eyes and then glanced down at the ground as she kicked the dirt and said, "My teacher told me not to worry about going to college, because I will never go anyway."

Words cannot express how I felt at that moment. I was absolutely stunned. Then I asked her, very concerned, "Did your teacher really tell you that?"

She nodded and said, "Yes!"

I told her that she could do whatever she wanted to do in life. If she wanted to go to college, then all she needed to do was study hard to make the grades to get in. She smiled, and in an instant it seemed like my words took root in her. My words of encouragement appeared to have inspired her to reach for something higher, as her smile gleamed from ear to ear. These words uplifted her, and it was as if I was witnessing her mind shift first-hand. That moment was very special to me.

Following our conversation, I started to share the same message of encouragement with all of the other young girls around me.

As a child, I was very fortunate to have a mom who always told me, "You can be anything you want to be" and "If they can do it, then so can you." My mother's words of encouragement gave me the confidence to reach for the stars despite any obstacles along the way.

It was such a great feeling to share her message of encouragement with the young girls that day. I loved being able to touch their lives in a positive way.

> *"Magic is believing in yourself, if you can do that,*
> *you can make anything happen."*
> –Johann Wolfgang von Goethe

You may be wondering what these examples have to do with money. Well, let's take a look at the words you are using toward money. Are they positive or negative? Because the words you speak are so powerful, it's important to understand the words you use today.

How would you categorize (positive or negative) the words you speak about your finances right now? Some of us may not view the words we speak about our finances to be positive or negative. But they tend to reflect how you think and feel about your financial situation. Here are some examples that I have categorized:

Positive
- "I'm going to be a millionaire one day."
- "We are creating businesses for our children's future."
- "I am planning and working toward an early retirement."
- "I plan to be debt-free in the next three years."
- "I would like to be financially independent someday."

Negative
- "I can't afford that!"
- "I'm broke!"
- "I have too many bills and just can't manage to keep up."
- "The only way to have money is to be an athlete or celebrity."
- "I'll never get out of debt!"

Suze Orman, in her book *The Courage to Be Rich*, shares some useful insight on the power of words:

> *Sometimes—with all of us—words just pop out, or we say something before we've thought it through, but when it comes to money, listen to the words you use. If you slip, simply take it back. Say, "I didn't mean that." Rephrase what you've said to reflect what you want to be true. Align your words with your goal, remembering the power in each and every word.*[5]

Think about the words you say about your finances. If they're negative, then start speaking more positively about money. Remember there is power in the words we speak, so use them to deliver your desires in life. The words we use reflect our thoughts, so it's important to take note of the types of words you choose. For you to develop the right mindset and drive the change you want, you will need to think, act, and speak more positively about your finances.

The way we think becomes our voice, what we say turns into action, and all of this combined turns into our life. The beauty of this process is that it begins with our state of mind. It is important to understand how you truly feel about money, what your thoughts are about it, and what you say about it. Having this awareness and bringing those elements into complete alignment will help you develop the right mindset and transform your life.

"Believe you can and you're halfway there."
–Theodore Roosevelt

---

5   Suze Orman, *The Courage to be Rich*, (New York: Riverhead Trade, 2001), 32.

Key Summary

- Look forward . . . just let go of your past mistakes and change what you're doing to drive the results you desire.

- Develop the right mindset to take you where you want to go.

- Have a "can do" attitude.

- Be positive in your thoughts and with the words you speak!

Key #2

ESTABLISH YOUR VISION AND GOALS

"Where there is no vision, the people perish."
–Proverbs 29:18 (King James Version)

Your vision is where you want to be in life. Do you have a vision? Having a clear vision of where you want to be is essential. And setting and achieving meaningful goals helps you realize your vision. After all, your goals are the stepping stones to get you there.

Create Your Vision

"Vision is the art of seeing what is invisible to others."
–Jonathan Swift

As you press forward with the right mindset, you must create your vision for where you want to be tomorrow. Because having a vision is instrumental in achieving success. Imagine that!

You hear it time and time again from people who have "made it." They usually say they envisioned their success before it actually happened. In other words, they had a vision for where they wanted to be. A great example of this was at the 2009 Academy Awards show when Kate Winslet won the Best Actress Oscar. It was a monumental moment for her, and she delivered a moving acceptance speech.

Winslet told the audience a story from her childhood. As a little girl, she had envisioned winning the Oscar. In fact, she'd started preparing her acceptance speech when she was about eight years old. She described to the audience how she had practiced her speech in front of the bathroom mirror, holding a shampoo bottle in place of the golden statuette. All these years later, here she was, with a real Oscar in place of the shampoo. She triumphantly declared that she had finally made it. Yes, her vision as a little girl had finally been realized.

If you want to change where you are today, you need a vision for where you want to be tomorrow. You may have many visions for different areas of your life—spiritual, family, personal, or financial. For the purposes of this book, we will focus on creating your financial vision. The following questions will help you think about where you want to be financially:
- When it comes to money, what would you like to improve on?
- Do you want to raise your credit score?
- Are you trying to save for a new home?
- Are you seeking to become financially independent?

A vision must be meaningful to you. It is important to document your vision and create one that truly reflects your desires and feelings. Some financial vision examples are:
- Become debt-free in the next five years.

- Reach financial independence by the age of forty and retire.
- Become a multi-millionaire.

Take a moment and really think about what your financial vision will be. Consider the following questions as you create your vision:
- What are your financial goals?
- What could you change about your finances today to make your future brighter?
- When you think of the word "money," what thoughts come to mind? What type of vision would drastically improve these thoughts?

Keep in mind that your vision may change based on your experiences and any life-changing events. And that's OK; just revisit your vision and make sure it reflects your desires. Your vision should be clear and concise and have meaning to you.

Let's get started. Create your personal financial vision here:

Now that you have created your vision, it is important to set goals to help you reach it. These may be a mix of short-term, mid-term, and long-term goals:

- A short-term goal is one that is targeted for completion within a year. For example, it may be as short as one day, or it may be several months.
- A mid-term goal ranges from one to three years.
- A long-term goal is one that you set for three years or longer.

Setting goals enables you to dig a little deeper into what you're trying to accomplish. Goals are specific actions (stepping stones) you need to take to achieve success.

The following example shows you a simple way to relate your vision to goals:

Your friend invites you to a party in Miami. The party will be on a Friday and starts at 6:00 p.m. You live in Jacksonville, 350 miles away. You try to get Thursday and Friday off work, but you're only able to get Friday off. You decide to drive to Miami and attend the party. You want to leave early enough to have some time to rest before the party, and you plan to spend Friday night there.

Your vision is: *To attend your friend's party in Miami.*

Your short-term goals may be as follows:

- Pack everything the night before the trip.
- Fill up and check the car ahead of time.
- Set the alarm to wake up early.
- Leave by 8:00 a.m. on Friday.

As you can see, by reaching all of your goals above, you are more likely to achieve your vision. For simplicity's sake, this example is very short-term focused. As I said before, your financial vision may require a mix of short-term, mid-term, and long-term goals.

When setting your goals, it is important to confirm that each goal aligns with your vision. If a goal doesn't align, you may want to reconsider the goal or revisit your vision statement to make sure it is still accurate.

Set Your Goals

"The greater danger for most of us is not that our aim is too high and we miss it, but that it is too low and we hit it."
– **Michelangelo**

Many successful people have invested time into setting goals for what they wanted to achieve in life. By setting and working toward those goals, ordinary people have accomplished extraordinary things.

Dr. Ben Carson, a renowned neurosurgeon, is a wonderful example of this. His uplifting book *Gifted Hands* tells how he overcame the odds against him and achieved success. And it shows you how an ordinary person can accomplish truly extraordinary things when he works toward his goals.

What's so amazing about Dr. Carson's story is that, as a young child, he was considered one of the worst students in his class. Despite this truth, he still dreamed of becoming a doctor one day. In *Gifted Hands*, he says: "Strangely enough, Mother started holding those **goals** in front of me when I wasn't a good student. No, that's not exactly true. I was the worst student in my whole fifth-grade class at Higgins Elementary School."[6]

Dr. Carson's story is a remarkable one. It shows us the importance of having a vision in spite of what your circumstances may be. And it reveals the power of setting goals and having the courage to relentlessly reach for them.

Dr. Carson's mother was his inspiration. She was a single parent who worked two or three jobs at a time to support her family. Although she had only a third-grade education and worked domestic jobs, she was very smart and took advantage of the opportunity to learn from her wealthy employers. She was a very loving and hopeful mother with strong faith, who encouraged her son Ben to reach for something higher in life. She understood what it took to be successful and worked hard with her children to instill in them a "can do" attitude, which gave them the confidence to accomplish anything in life. She set goals, and her kids worked toward those goals, taking the needed actions to accomplish them. Those actions included limiting the amount of television they watched, reading more books, and writing weekly book reports.

The hard work and effort paid off with unbelievable results, as her son went from being the worst student in his class to the top student in just a few years. He eventually graduated from Yale University and the University of Michigan's medical school. Most importantly, he realized his vision of being a doctor. Dr. Carson is a well-respected doctor in neuroscience, and by age thirty-three he was the director of pediatric neurosurgery at Johns Hopkins Medical Institute.

---

6   Taken from *Gifted Hands* by Ben Carson, Copyright © 1990 by Review and Herald Publishing Association. Used by permission of Zondervan. www.zondervan.com.

Dr. Carson understands the importance of setting goals and achieving them. He is passionate about helping others succeed and works with kids on how to set and reach their goals in life.

Here are several tips to help you create your goals:

- **Start by setting SMART goals.** Align the right mindset with your vision and goals. Your new way of thinking may enhance your vision, and that's OK. Keeping everything in complete alignment is very important in realizing your vision and goals. So, let's aim to shoot higher in life but always remember to set SMART goals.

SMART	DEFINITION	GOAL EXAMPLE
Specific	A specific goal is explicit about what you are trying to accomplish. It is easy to understand, clear, and concise.	My first novel will be published by summer 2015.
Measurable	The goal must be measureable. Is it something that you can gauge your progress against?	I will be debt-free on January 1, 2014.
Attainable	The goal must be within reach. It has to be something that is achievable.	I will be financially independent in five years by owning my own business and building wealth through investments.
Relevant	This verifies the goal is in alignment with your vision. Is this goal relevant to what you are trying to accomplish overall?	Pay off all my credit card debt by the end of the year.
Timely	Set target dates for reaching your goals. Depending on the complexity of the goal, you may want to set milestones; this can be used to signify the progress made toward reaching your goal.	I want to attend a financial seminar at least three times a year to improve my financial knowledge and stay abreast of changes in the industry.

- **After you have created your SMART goals, make notes on the actions you will take to reach each goal.** These actions are critical steps in accomplishing your goals. You may consider creating a specific time frame around some of your actions to recognize them as milestones. A milestone is a point in time when you will complete a certain action. For example, if I had Dr. Carson's goal of becoming a doctor, my milestones might be:
  - Graduate from undergraduate school with a bachelor's degree in 2015.
  - Graduate from medical school in 2019.
  - Complete hospital residency in 2024.

- **Keep your goals in front of you and monitor your progress.** It is important to write your goals down and remember them. If you have them in front of you, you will be more likely to put forth the effort to reach them. For instance, some people write them on a piece of paper and hang them on their bathroom mirror so they can see them every day. I have heard of others taping their goals on the ceiling to remind them every day when they wake up. Others write them on a notepad and schedule time to review their goals and progress monthly or quarterly. How you do it is up to you. The point is to write them down and keep them where you can be reminded of what you are working to accomplish.

I remember when my husband and I first started dating. I asked him about his long-term goals in life. His response was more than I could have fathomed at the time.

He said, "My goal is to retire by the age of forty."

I thought that was a magnificent goal. However, the other day, when I reminded him of our discussion he said, "Oh well, I don't remember that. I'd better get started working on that now." It has been more than a decade since we had that initial conversation, and he is only a few years away from forty, saying he needs to get started on his plan. Had he been more diligent in keeping his goal in front of him and tracking his progress, he could have easily assessed whether he was on track. Nonetheless, I believe in him and I am sure he will accomplish whatever he sets out to do.

"Energy is the essence of life. Every day you decide how you're going to use it by knowing what you want and what it takes to reach that goal, and by maintaining focus."
–Oprah Winfrey

- **Visualize yourself accomplishing your goals.** Visualization is a key element in reaching your goals. Many successful musicians often tell how they imagined themselves where they are now before it actually happened. Visualization is the art of seeing yourself accomplishing something before you actually do.

  For example, during my junior year in college I had a goal of buying my first car that summer. I told my close friends and family that I was getting a car, but in reality, the odds did not look very favorable. So many people doubted me. After all, I didn't have a driver's license and my mother surely wasn't going to pay for a car. Yet, I saw myself getting the car and driving it back to school my senior year. People were pretty shocked when it actually happened!

- **Set aside time to revisit your goals and track your success against your target dates.** This will give you a sense of per-

41

sonal accountability and accomplishment as you work toward and achieve your goals.

- **If you are married or have a significant other and both of you work together as one on your financial obligations, set your goals together and hold each other accountable for the results.** For those who are single, it may be helpful to have someone close to you hold you accountable for achieving your goals. If you need support, ask someone you trust or seek out a coach to help you. Having an accountability partner could help keep you motivated. You could make it like a buddy system, in which each of you sets your goals, encourages each other, and tracks the progress you're making together.

- **Take the time to celebrate your successes along the way to realizing your vision.** It may be a simple outing like going to the movies or going out to dinner. It does not have to be anything extravagant, but rewarding yourself for achieving a goal can help motivate you to press forward on your journey toward your ultimate vision.

> *"The secret to productive goal setting is in establishing clearly defined goals, writing them down and then focusing on them several times a day with words, pictures, and emotions as if we've already achieved them."*
> –Denis Waitley

Now that you know how to create your vision and set your goals, let's take a look at a couple of real stories that show you how it's done.

Renee's Story

Renee learned about money from her parents. Unfortunately, they demonstrated poor money management habits. Her mother used credit cards to fund dream vacations, shopped frequently, and had problems keeping up with the bills that came along with her lifestyle. Renee adopted some of her mother's spending habits, going on occasional shopping sprees, buying more than $400 worth of clothes in just one shopping trip. All of the shopping really started adding up. She bought so many clothes that some of them were never worn and still had tags on them. Her spending habits eventually landed her in thousands of dollars of credit card debt, so much that she had to claim bankruptcy a few years later. In Renee's mind, she just had too much debt and saw no way out.

Several years after declaring bankruptcy she managed to get back into credit card debt. You see, bankruptcy did not change her spending behavior, and if the root cause is not addressed then you're bound to repeat it.

After watching Renee struggle with her finances, I reached out to her to see if she needed help. We met and discussed her vision and the goals she had for her finances. Then we worked together to create a plan to achieve those goals.

Her vision was to drastically improve her financial situation and gain control of her finances. The goals we set together to achieve that vision were:

- Eliminate her debt, except student loans.
- Increase her income.
- Improve her credit score.
- Save money for the future.

We also laid out the actions she would take to accomplish these goals.

- Eliminate her debt, except student loans:
  - Participate in the development of her debt-free action plan by finding out the balances and interest rates on her debt.
  - Refinance car for a lower interest rate.
  - Adhere to the debt-free action plan.
  - Be accountable to her financial coach (me) for reaching goals.

- Increase her income:
  - Go back to school to get the needed skills to get a higher paying job.
  - Apply for school and seek out any available scholarships.
  - Graduate from school and start a new career.

- Improve her credit score:
  - Pay bills on time.
  - Limit spending to items that she needs and can pay for.
  - Keep her car longer and use her regular car payment money to pay off other debt.
  - Avoid cosigning for anyone.

- Build a savings account:
  - Open a savings account.
  - Regularly contribute a portion of her income to savings and access this money only for emergency situations.

Renee was committed to her plan and determined to succeed. It took some time to achieve some of her goals, but she accomplished each and every one of them:

- She paid off all of her debt, except the student loans. Renee paid off the credit cards one by one and cancelled high-interest-rate credit cards. She also managed to pay off her car a year and a half early.

- She went to school and maintained her full-time day job. She graduated and started a new rewarding career.
- She drastically improved her credit score to be over 700.
- She also did something she never felt possible, which was to build a savings account. It was unbelievable, because she managed to put away thousands of dollars while paying down debt. It was her determination, self-control, and discipline that enabled her to achieve all of her financial goals.

My Financial Vision

When I found out that I was pregnant with my first child, I created a new financial vision that focused on paying off all of my debt (excluding our mortgage) before my daughter was born. Having friends who had kids, I knew that we would have new expenses to account for monthly, and doing this would better position my husband and me for them. My financial vision was to:

Eliminate my personal debt (student loans and auto loan) before my new baby arrived on August 12, 2003 (my due date).

This was a short-term vision, given that a baby normally arrives in nine months. Given the short time frame, it was critical that I develop realistic goals and chart my progress regularly.

The goals and actions I outlined to support my vision were:
- Capture the details of my outstanding debt:
  - interest rates
  - payoff amounts

- Develop a debt-free action plan:
  - Outline my payoff strategy:

- Determine which assets (e.g., savings, stocks) to use.
- Lay out the steps I would take to reach my goal, including target dates and monthly payments.

- Pay off the highest-interest-rate items first while continuing to pay on the other items. For example, if I had student loan with 6% interest, and my auto loan is at 5% interest, I would pay the extra money on the student loan and continue paying my normal payment on the auto loan. Once I completely paid off the student loan, I would pay extra money on the outstanding auto loan.

- Pay off debts by August 1, 2003:
  - Confirm that all of my target completion dates enable me to reach this goal.

The goals I set were instrumental in realizing my financial vision. I included my husband in creating my vision, goals, and actions. I don't know if he truly believed I would reach it, but given the projected weekly daycare costs ($190+), he was on board for the ride.

I worked diligently to track my payments and enjoyed watching the balances go down. It really kept me motivated! Managing my expenses diligently helped me minimize the debt I had to pay off. For example, I always paid off my credit card bills monthly. Therefore, my debt consisted of only four student loans and an auto loan, which normally have lower interest rates than credit cards. As an avid saver, I was able to set realistic goals because I knew I could use savings and sell some of my company stock to reach my goals.

In less than seven months, I paid off more than $20,000 in debt. It was nice to drive my car without a car note and to receive my car title in the mail. This gave me a real sense of accomplishment. As for the student loans, it was a great feeling to have finally paid them off, because the monthly payment was so high that it seemed like another car note. Most importantly, paying off debt gives you more financial freedom. It also gave me more peace of mind with the new expenses that came along with our little bundle of joy.

There are many life events that bring us happiness and test our money management skills. Later in the book we will revisit debt ("Key #5: Drop the Debt Weight") and spending habits ("Key #4: Live Below Your Means to Get Ahead"). Because most of the time, major life events impact our financial picture, and it is how we respond to these events that matters most.

Now that you have a few examples, start writing your goals. To get started, you can use the table on the next page to capture your goals (i.e., actions, target dates).

"If you want to be happy, set a goal that commands your thoughts, liberates your energy, and inspires your hopes."
–Andrew Carnegie

#	GOAL DESCRIPTION	ACTION(S)	TARGET DATE	COMMENTS
1	Example: Pay off student loans	Get payoff amounts and create payoff plan	12/31/2016	

Key Summary

- Create your financial vision for where you want to be and write it down.

- Set SMART goals. Focus on how you will accomplish your goals and invest the time in documenting the actions you will take to reach them.

- Be sure your mindset, vision, and goals align for the best results.

- Visualize yourself achieving your goals.

- Track your progress along the way. Consider asking someone you trust to hold you accountable.

- Remember to celebrate your accomplishments along the way!

Key #3

WATCH WHERE YOUR MONEY GOES . . . LITERALLY!

"The art is not in making money, but in keeping it."
– Proverb

Shortly after I left my company, I was at a big business event and I started to discuss my decision to leave with a couple of other women. They were both happy to hear about my decision to pursue my dream of helping everyday people improve their personal finances.

In their minds, the need could not have been greater, given we were in the midst of "The Great Recession." Managing money had come to the top of everyone's attention given the number of layoffs. So, as you can imagine, talking about personal finance seemed to raise everyone's energy level.

In fact, it showed on one woman's face as her cheeks started to blush and her smile widened from ear to ear. Then she raised her arms and opened them wide to dramatize her question for me. She asked, "OK, OK, if you could offer someone only one financial tip, what would it be?"

I thought about her question for only a few moments. Then I responded, "If I could offer up one piece of financial advice, it would be to watch where your money goes!"

She continued smiling and nodded her head in agreement.

And the other woman agreed too. In fact, she then told us how she had discovered she was being overcharged for her medical benefits while out on maternity leave. During her leave, she had decided to take some time to review her paycheck stubs, and that's how she found out she was paying too much money for her insurance.

She couldn't believe her eyes and went back pay period after pay period to determine how long it had been happening. Next, she gathered everything and called the payroll and benefits department to discuss the issue. The department was helpful and took note of her concerns. Unfortunately, as with many financial issues, the problem was not resolved immediately in one phone conversation. The person she spoke with opened up a case to have the problem investigated further.

The investigation confirmed the issue. Thankfully, the problem was corrected on her next paycheck, and she also received a full refund for the previous payroll deduction errors. She still could not believe it had happened at all, especially for so long.

She ended her story with great emphasis, saying, "You definitely have to watch where your money goes!"

I learned the importance of watching where your money goes when I worked as a personal banking specialist at a regional bank in the South. Working in retail banking gave me an opportunity to increase my personal finance knowledge, in areas such as financial products, terminology, and rules. But the most valuable experience I took away from this job was in the lessons I learned from my banking customers.

Although the bank had customers from all walks of life, they could generally be segmented into two groups based on their financial behaviors. It was very interesting to observe how differently customers from each group handled their money.

I'll refer to the first group of customers as extremely money conscious—when it came to money, they had a heightened awareness. Many of the customers in this group were rich. And the common trait among them was their close attention to detail in money management. They had an impeccable ability to keep a close eye on every penny that was spent. My interactions with them were primarily to verify that their checkbooks balanced properly or to discuss bank charges. These customers would complain about any bank charges, no matter how small the amount—even if it was just a dollar. I quickly learned that these customers were very detail oriented and certainly knew where their money went.

The extremely money conscious customers were very knowledgeable in managing their finances. And no matter how large their balances may have been, they still managed to stay on top of each and every dollar and cent they had. They were also very upbeat and positive about life (remember mindset). Many of them had strong desires to help others. In fact, they often shared their secrets for success and words of wisdom with me, occasionally offering unsolicited advice on life and business. These customers appeared to be compassionate people, as they told me about their generous acts of kindness.

On the flip side, the second group of customers was a mix of people across all income levels. This group was much larger (about 90% of the customers I interacted with on a daily basis) than the first and included your typical banking customers. I provided these customers with more of a variety of services such as balance inquiries and other general banking transactions (transfers, transaction verifications, opening and closing of accounts). However, most of these customers would be checking their balances or calling because their accounts were overdrawn.

For those of you unfamiliar with banking terms, an overdrawn account is one with a negative balance, so money is owed. An account is overdrawn when you spend more money than you have in the account. Unlike the first group, these customers rarely questioned any bank charges, such as overdrawn check fees (roughly $30 each at the time, more today) or ATM fees that may have ranged from $1–$5 per withdrawal.

Contrary to the first group, they monitored their accounts more loosely and would ask for their balances instead of telling me what they should be. And they were less familiar with how their accounts worked. Some of them lost more money in bank charges than they earned in interest on their savings accounts.

Working at the bank shed light on the challenges many people faced managing their money. It was sad to see seniors living on fixed incomes with so many overdrawn check fees that a good portion of their monthly Social Security checks paid for bank fees. They were struggling to make ends meet, and you could sense their hopelessness. It was difficult to watch people losing their hard-earned money in this way. I tried to help them as best as I could, but they felt there was no way out.

Robert's Story

Robert expects to get his Social Security check next week and decides to check his account balance before going out to run some errands. He calls the bank only to be told that his account is overdrawn by $245.

He asks when his Social Security check is normally deposited and confirms the exact payment amount. Then he thanks the bank representative and hurries off the phone.

While the story above is hypothetical, it is drawn from reality. There are many people just like Robert out there, anxiously waiting for a deposit. Robert is less likely to question any bank charges or the accuracy of his account balance. Instead, he awaits his next Social Security deposit to bring his account into the positive.

If Robert receives a $650 Social Security deposit, he could find himself trying to live on $405 for the entire month after the bank collects the money owed on his account (including bank fees). This is how the cycle starts, because he has to spend more than he makes every month just to keep up with everyday expenses, while the bank fees keep adding up when he overdraws his account.

These are the customers I had to refrain from asking, "Do you know how much money you are wasting every month in bank fees?" The scariest part was that they already knew it, and you could hear the sound of defeat in their voices. Sadly, it had been accepted as a way of life. These are the people I wanted to help educate so I could make a difference in the quality of their lives.

That's why watching where your money goes is one of the most important lessons in money management. After all, it's your money.

I encourage you to master this principle, because any time you are more attentive to something, it performs better or lasts longer. How would you like to see your money last longer and perform better?

You can only control what's within your control.
And when you do this well, you'll see the
BIG difference it makes in your life.

Where to Start Watching

The best place to start watching where your money goes is your paycheck. When is the last time you checked your paystub? If you haven't checked it, how do you know you are being paid correctly?

To properly check your pay, you have to know how much you make. That may sound simple, but a lot of people don't know exactly how much they're supposed to be paid.

The calculation is easier when you're paid hourly. Your gross wages, listed on your paystub, are calculated using your total hours (worked in the pay period) multiplied by your hourly rate. For example, if you worked eighty-eight hours in the pay period and make $12.00 per hour, then your paystub would reflect the following:

88 hours x $12.00 hourly rate = $1,056 gross earnings

Your gross earnings are the total amount earned without taxes or any other payroll deductions (e.g., stock purchase, retirement accounts, benefits). It is important to confirm that your hours worked and hourly rate are both correct when you check your pay.

If you have a salaried job, you will have to understand how your pay cycle works to confirm whether you're being paid correctly. For example, I used to get paid twice a month, which amounted to twenty-four times a year. I verified my income by taking my salary and dividing it by twenty-four pay periods. This calculation assumed I worked full time or used paid time off (e.g., vacation, sick time) during each pay period. The example below shows what a paycheck calculation for a salaried employee may look like for a given pay period:

PAY PERIOD: 4/16/2011 - 4/30/2011		
Pay Type	Pay Period Hours	Total Pay
Normal Pay	88	$2,741.81

Be sure to direct any payroll questions or issues you may have to your payroll or human resources department. They should be able to walk you through how your wages are calculated and distributed. It's important for you to understand the calculation to confirm whether you're being paid correctly.

Being more proactive in checking your pay helps ensure you make the money you earned. You can do this by setting aside a little time every month to review your paystubs.

Everyone can make a mistake, even your employer. I remember when I found a payroll error myself. It happened when I was expecting to receive one of my biggest pay raises. I was so happy about my new salary and couldn't wait to check my paystub. Good thing I did, because it was wrong! My paystub did not reflect my new salary at all. I checked it multiple times to make sure I was right.

I contacted the payroll department to tell them about the problem. We confirmed my salary on record and walked through the calculation together on the call. Sure enough, there was an error. The good news is that the issue was corrected the next pay period, when I received the corrected payroll calculation and the additional pay I was owed from the prior pay period. I don't know whether my employer would have caught this payroll issue, but I was sure glad I had. After all, who cares more about your money than you?

After you verify your gross earnings, check your deductions. I know you may be saying, what? But you have to make sure your deductions are right. There are different types of deductions on your paystub, and these deductions may be made with pre-tax or after-tax dollars. A pre-tax deduction is taken out before your earnings are taxed. Some examples of pre-tax deductions are:

- Medical benefits
- Retirement account (e.g., 401(k))
- Flexible spending accounts (e.g., daycare)

After-tax deductions are taken after your earnings are taxed. Some examples of after-tax deductions are:

- Charity donation
- Insurance (e.g., life, long-term disability coverage)
- Company stock deductions

You may be saying those are a lot of deductions to consider. Well, you're right. But an easy way to check them is to use a copy of your benefits summary. When you sign up for benefits (insurance, retirement contributions), you usually receive a summary that shows you how much money will be deducted from your pay each pay period. If you do not have a benefits summary, your employer should have a copy available for you on record.

Use the amounts on your benefits summary to check your payroll deductions. If the amounts are higher or lower than expected, call your benefits office to find out why. If they are too low, you may not be receiving the benefits you signed up for, and if they are too high, you could be over-paying.

Also, keep a copy of any other payroll deductions you agree to, such as any charitable donation pledges you may have made. Make it a habit to check any new payroll deductions you sign up for to ensure they are being taken out of your paycheck correctly.

Your federal income tax withholdings also deduct money from your pay. Your W-4, which you are responsible for filling out for your employer, determines how much money is taken out. If you always receive a large annual tax refund from the Internal Revenue Service (IRS), it may be worth reviewing your W-4 for accuracy. That money you are getting back is money you could be using throughout the year as additional income versus having the government keep it for you interest-free. For some people, it may be a conscious decision to treat your taxes like a savings account and receive this extra money back annually. You should understand this decision essentially takes money out of your pocket during the rest of the year—money that is not accruing any interest.

Another reason to review your W-4 and make any needed changes is if you have a life-changing event like marriage, a new child, or divorce.

Use the IRS withholding calculator to help you determine whether you need to change your W-4 form. You can find this tool on www.irs.gov. This calculator could help you avoid paying too much or too little in federal income taxes.

If you are interested in verifying your state tax and other tax-related payroll deductions (e.g., Federal Insurance Contributions Act, or FICA), then I'd suggest you contact your payroll department for more information on how these amounts are calculated. They are usually percentage-based calculations.

I rarely check all of the tax figures, but if you want to, that's awesome! Several years back, I discovered a state tax issue where I had unknowingly paid taxes to a state that I never lived or worked in. So, it's definitely possible for these types of errors to occur too. And the earlier you catch them, the better, because in my case, I ended up having to file state taxes in the state I never lived or worked in.

Checking your pay will get easier to do after you understand how it is calculated. Then, you can start reviewing it monthly. It should take you fifteen minutes tops per pay period once you get the hang of it.

Investing the time upfront to check your pay will help ensure you are making the money you should be earning and save you money in payroll errors. In other words, checking your pay will keep more money in your pocket.

Bank Smart

These days, it's easier to get a bank account than ever. And the offers have come a long way from a toaster, like $125 cash to open an account. You receive offers in the mail, and sometimes they're out looking for you in the grocery store aisles.

I believe everyone should have an account, but you have to bank smart. Whether you choose to keep your money in a bank or with any other financial institution (e.g., credit union), you must be mindful of how you handle your finances. That's what I mean when I say bank smart.

Banking smart starts with the decisions you make. When it comes to the financial products (savings, checking) you're considering, be sure to understand the products first and shop around for the best deals that meet your needs. Most banks and credit unions offer you the following types of deposit accounts:

- **Checking**—A checking account allows you to write checks against the funds in your account. Checking accounts may be interest or non-interest bearing. These accounts usually provide you normal banking transactions such as transfers, deposits, and withdrawals, and many offer online banking. Online banking allows you to pay your bills automatically from the bank's website, saving you time and money. A checking account normally comes with an automated teller machine (ATM) or debit card. The ATM card allows you to withdraw money from your account any time. A debit card acts as an ATM and credit card (it usually has a Visa or MasterCard logo to provide you the convenience of a credit card). However, unlike credit cards, your debit card withdraws the funds directly from your account.

- **Savings**—A savings account is an interest-bearing account, meaning you earn money from your money. This account has certain types of withdrawal transaction limits. For example, federal regulations limit the number of withdrawals and/or transfers to six in a given monthly statement period for certain types of withdrawals. Most financial institutions allow ATM or debit cards to be used for withdrawals on savings accounts.

- **Money market**—A money market account is similar to a savings account in that it is interest bearing and has withdrawal transactions limits. These types of accounts usually pay higher interest rates than regular savings accounts, however they may require a higher minimum balance to avoid a monthly fee. Money market accounts usually offer check-writing privileges. Many financial institutions allow ATM cards to be used for withdrawals on money market accounts.

 TIP

There are federal regulations in place that limit the number of account withdrawals on some bank accounts (e.g., savings). Be sure to understand the details behind these limitations to avoid charges.

It's important to understand how your account works before you open it. Here are some questions you may want to consider:
- What is required to avoid the monthly service fee (minimum balance requirement, direct deposit, minimum bank transactions)?
- Are there any withdrawal transaction limits? If so, what are they? And, what happens if you exceed them?
- Can you withdraw money from your account without any penalty fees?
- Are there any specific customer-service-related fees? For example, do they charge you for in-person service from a bank representative or teller?
- What benefits (e.g., free checks, notary services, traveler's checks) do you receive as a customer?

- Do they offer any account package deals? For example, will you receive any additional savings or discounts for having more than one account (mortgage, credit card, savings)? If so, how do the deals work? Are there minimum balance requirements?
- What fees or limitations do you have with an ATM or debit card? (Be sure to consider the number of ATM locations they have available in your area to save on these fees.)
- Do they offer overdraft protection? If so, how does it work? What are the costs associated with these bank services? (Overdraft protection transfers money into your account from another source such as savings or a credit card to prevent your account from being overdrawn.)
- What type of account notifications do they provide (e-mail, text)? (Hopefully, these notifications are included free.)
- Do they offer telephone, online, or mobile banking services? If so, how much does it cost?
- Do they offer automatic savings transfers? (This would enable you to automatically transfer money from your checking into savings at a specified time.) If so, how does it work and are there any fees?
- Bank: Will the Federal Deposit Insurance Corporation (FDIC) insure your account? If so, up to what dollar amount?
- Credit union: Will the National Credit Union Administration (NCUA) insure your account? If so, up to what dollar amount?

IMPORTANT

The FDIC and NCUA insure deposits up to a specific amount. "The Federal Deposit Insurance Corporation (FDIC) preserves and promotes public confidence in the U.S. financial system by insuring deposits in banks and thrift institutions for at least

$250,000."[7] The NCUA insures deposits in federally insured credit unions up to $250,000 per individual depositor. These limits are at the time of this writing; be sure to check with the financial institution for the latest coverage amounts.

It's a good idea to compare different financial institutions to find the best account for you. Also consider their locations, customer service, and any other meaningful criteria you may have to make your final selection.

When you bank smart you can save money on bank fees, because you'll be more aware of what it takes to avoid monthly service charges. For example, you will be more likely to meet the direct deposit requirement or maintain the minimum balance to avoid the monthly service fee. More importantly, you'll choose the account that's right for you from the start. After all, the goal is to save and protect your money.

 TIP

Credit unions are financial institutions you may want to consider for your banking needs. Credit unions may offer you more savings (e.g., free checking) and better interest rates (e.g., loans, deposit accounts).

Once you've set up your account, watch out for changes. Financial institutions occasionally modify their products, and sometimes these changes could negatively impact you. New federal regulation requirements, bank mergers, and acquisitions may change the way your account works. So it's important to stay up to date on any new account changes to avoid surprises (e.g., new charges).

---

7   Federal Deposit Insurance Corporation website. Accessed June 6, 2011.
    http://www.fdic.gov/about/learn/symbol/index.html.

Be aware of account change notifications and read any communication you may receive. If you need any clarification, contact your financial institution for assistance.

Effectively Manage Your Account

To effectively manage your account, you must balance your account to ensure everything adds up correctly and check for any transaction errors. It is important to get in the habit of doing this every month, because there are time limitations for when the bank is responsible for resolving errors. So it's best to contact your bank immediately if you identify any problems.

Balancing your account is easier today, because online banking gives you 24/7 access to your account activity. Plus, many financial institutions provide you with step-by-step instructions on how to balance your account right on the back of your account statement. Have you ever noticed that?

You can start balancing your account now. From this point forward, monitor your account balance and confirm your transactions (deposits, withdrawals). You balance your account by:

1. Taking your last account statement balance
2. Adding any deposits (e.g., direct deposits) or credits since your last statement
3. Subtracting any withdrawal transactions (e.g., checks, deposits, ATM withdrawals, withdrawals (e.g., automatic, debit card), or other withdrawal activity (fees) since your last account statement
4. The account balances when the new account balance on your next statement equals your calculated account balance. For example, if your last statement balance was $500 and your transactions since that statement included: $250 deposit, $100 check, $50 withdrawal, and $25 debit card purchase. Add up all

credits ($250) to the last account balance ($500) and subtract all debits (check, withdrawal, and debit card, totaling $175). If all transactions posted to your account, the new statement balance should be $575.

 TIP

When you receive your account statement, confirm all your deposits and withdrawal transactions that have posted are correct. You can verify your transactions (amount, vendor, and other relevant information) using your monthly statement or in real time using online access to identify any posting errors.

While your account balance may differ from your financial institution's version of your balance with outstanding transactions, you should still be able to verify your account balance using the transactions that have already posted to your account. If you find any discrepancies during your review, be sure to bring them to your financial institution's attention immediately.

I know we are in the information age, but errors can still occur. For example, I made an ATM deposit that was never credited to my account. After checking my account the following day to verify the transaction, I noticed the problem. My bank asked me to give it a few more days. However, after several days it still hadn't posted to my account, and they couldn't find it, so I had to file a missing deposit report and request a new check to be issued. If I hadn't bothered to check, I could have lost my deposit without even knowing it.

It's true that mistakes can happen, even with online banking. Although the likelihood of these types of errors may be minimal, there's still a chance. You might pay your bill online, and that company never receives the payment. I remember speaking with a customer who had a major issue with his account being overdrawn. We found out that the problem happened because his $50 monthly gym membership had posted for $500. That extra zero made a big difference in his account, and he promptly contacted us to resolve the issue. This type of error could have gone unnoticed had he not been paying attention to his account.

When you effectively manage your account, you're protecting your money. If you don't, you are essentially leaving it up to everyone else.

Be Credit Wise

> *"Remember that credit is money."*
> **–Benjamin Franklin**

As a mathematic equation: CREDIT = MONEY. Despite any of the attractive marketing materials you may receive, there is a cost to using credit, unless you pick a no-annual-fee credit card and pay your balance in full when it's due.

Credit Cards
The most popular form of credit is a credit card. And like any other financial product, you need to have a good understanding of the terms, fees, and rules to choose the card that's right for you. Here's a list of common credit card charges and fees that you may consider:

- **Annual fee**—An annual fee is a yearly fee that you must pay to have the credit card. If your credit card has no annual fee, review your bill to verify you are not charged.
- **Over-the-limit fee**—This fee is charged when you permit your credit card company to charge you for exceeding the credit

card limit. For example, you have a credit limit of $500, and you charge $525. I'd recommend not permitting your credit card company to charge this fee.

- **Late fee**—A late fee is assessed when you do not pay your credit card bill on time. If you're having problems paying on time, consider setting up automatic bill payments.
- **Returned payment fee**—This fee is charged when the payment you make is returned back from your financial institution unpaid.
- **Cash advance fee**—The amount charged for taking out cash on your card.
- **Balance transfer fee**—This is a fee that the credit card company charges you when you transfer another credit card balance onto your card. Pay attention to the fine print on any credit card balance transfer offers you receive, so you have a full understanding of the terms and charges.
- **Annual percentage rate/interest rate**—The interest rate is a percentage-based calculation that your lender uses to calculate the charges for money borrowed (outstanding balance owed) on your account. Interest rates may be fixed or variable. See the bullet on finance charge below for more details on the types of interest rates.
- **Default rate**—Be sure to understand what this rate means on your card and what triggers it to go into effect. These rates can be as high as more than 30% interest. They usually kick in with a missed or late payment, so beware of it and try to avoid it.
- **Finance charge**—When choosing your card, always remember credit card companies make money when you don't pay your balance in full each month. This is the finance charge. The actual amount charged is based on your interest rate. It is best to have a card with a low fixed rate, preferably less than 15%.

Here's more on rates. A **fixed rate** is a constant annual percentage rate that you are charged throughout the year. Although you may have a fixed rate credit card, keep in mind that this can change at your lender's discretion. Unlike fixed-rate cards, **your annual percentage rate can change with a variable interest rate card.**

Here's how interest is calculated. Fixed rate cards offer you a specific interest rate that does not change unless your credit card terms change. For example, you may be charged a fixed interest rate of 7.9% on purchases. On the other hand, variable interest rate calculations are usually based on a flat fixed value plus prime rate (standard financial rate). The prime rate is used to determine your variable credit card interest rate. The Federal Reserve sets the prime rate every quarter, and it is available to the public online or with your bank.

An example of a credit card offer with a variable interest rate may say:

> *The purchase annual percentage rate (APR) may vary monthly and equals the Prime Rate + 10%.*

In this example, you simply add the prime rate to flat fixed value of 10%. If prime is 3%, then your variable interest rate is 13% for the month.

I prefer fixed-rate cards to variable rates because it's easier to tell the true cost of credit over a given time period. However, most lenders offer variable interest rate cards.

Many companies try to entice you with irresistible credit offers such as a 0% introductory APR. Although this may sound attractive, be sure to take into consideration the length of the introductory rate period and the normal interest rate after the promotion. If you get a great offer like 0% APR for twelve months, it may definitely be worth considering.

Another factor you may want to consider is the credit card's benefits. Show me the benefits! Will you receive cash back, travel rewards/perks (without any blackout dates), savings for a college fund, or mortgage rewards? How about warranty protection or traveler's insurance? You'd be surprised by the different benefits credit cards can offer you. If you're comparing two credit cards, the benefits may be the deciding factor.

A few websites that will help you compare different credit cards are CreditCards.com, Bankrate.com, and CardTrak.com.

Check Your Credit Card Statement

Review your credit card statement every month. This will help you verify your account activity, such as credit card charges, credits, and payments. Using receipts makes it easier to check your transactions.

Another reason to review your monthly credit card statement is to identify any fraudulent account activity or errors. For example, I found over $3,000 worth of charges that I didn't make on my credit card one month. I quickly contacted my credit card company to open a fraud claim and received a new credit card. What if I hadn't bothered to check my account that month? I could have paid for someone else's shopping spree. And there was that time when my $5.94 sub sandwich posted for a whopping $594. Good thing I caught that mistake. What foot-long sub is worth paying over $500 for?

Also pay close attention to your interest rate. If you are supposed to receive a special introductory rate, check your statement to confirm you're receiving it for the specified period. You should be notified in advance of any interest rate changes. If you're not notified and you find a problem, then contact your credit card company to discuss it further.

For additional information on credit cards visit www.federalreserve.gov/creditcard.

Home Equity, Mortgage, and Other Loans

Always take the time to understand the financial terms and costs involved prior to securing any personal loans. For example, if you're applying for a mortgage, will there be a prepayment penalty? If it's an auto loan, what is your interest rate? Sometimes dealers want to focus on your car payment. But it's important for you to know the interest rate and term (e.g., sixty months) to make sure you're getting a competitive deal. Having this information upfront enables you to make the best financial decision for you.

I remember when we bought our first home and I reviewed the closing statement. I was surprised to see all of the little charges and fees that quickly added up. In fact, I found about $900 of them to be questionable. When I called to inquire about the charges, the organization could not explain any of them. So they were all removed before closing, saving me close to $1,000.

Review your monthly loan statements. Here are some tips to help you monitor your loans:
- Verify your payment posts to your account correctly.
- Check your outstanding balance. As you pay down your loan, the principal (amount owed) should be reduced.
- Verify your interest rate. For example, if you have a thirty-year mortgage with a 5% fixed interest rate, it should remain the

same throughout your term. The only way it should change is if you refinanced your home. If you have an adjustable-rate mortgage, then make sure any adjustments are within the specified interest rate range. For example, if it cannot exceed 3% in a given adjustment period, then your new rate should stay within that range.

- Confirm extra payments are applied correctly. Paying extra money on your principal helps you save more money in interest. But, some lenders require you to notify them in advance of how they should handle any extra payment amount, so be sure to follow the process. When you do not follow the process, you may find your extra payment being held and carried over to your next bill.

Student Loans

It's best to understand how student loans work before you take them. In 2010, it was reported for the first time that student loan debt exceeded outstanding credit card debt in the U.S. If you are a student considering taking out a loan, be sure to evaluate all of the options (grants, scholarships, federal and private student loans) available to pay for school.

You can start by applying for financial assistance. Visit www.fafsa.ed.gov for information on federal student aid. Also, FinAid.org is one of the best websites to help you find more information on your financial aid options. There are many types of student loans, such as Perkins, Stafford, PLUS, and private lenders. When comparing student loan options, consider the loan type (unsubsidized, subsidized, federal), repayment terms (interest rate and repayment period), and whether it offers loan forgiveness. It's important to choose a student loan that meets your needs best.

Here are a few tips to manage your student loan:

- Keep a copy of your student loan promissory note and any other loan information you receive from your school or lender. This will help you ensure the information pertaining to your loan is accurate. For example, you can check your actual interest rate and repayment period against the original terms of the loan to verify there are no discrepancies.
- Pay your student loans on time to avoid any fees and to keep your credit rating in good standing.
- Set up automatic student loan payments. This may lower your interest rate and give you more peace of mind.
- When student loan rates are very low (e.g., less than 3%), you may want to consider consolidating your federal student loans. Keep in mind the benefits that you may lose after consolidating your loans. For instance, my husband consolidated his student loans to receive a lower payment option over a longer period of time. While the payment was lower, he was paying a high interest rate of 9%. And when student loan rates went down to 4%, he was stuck with his high interest rate because he could not reconsolidate his loan. If you need a lower payment, talk with your lender. You may be able to get one without consolidating all of your loans.
- Your student loan interest may be tax deductible.
- Make extra payments (if you can) to pay off your student loans more quickly. This will save you money.
- If you're having problems paying your student loans, talk with your lender about more affordable repayment options (income-based repayment or an extended payment term). Depending on your circumstances, you may qualify for a loan deferment or forbearance. Be sure to get any new repayment agreements in writing. Keep in mind when you extend your repayment terms, your loan will cost you more money in in-

terest. However, if you're experiencing financial hardships that are preventing you from paying off your loan, these options should be carefully considered.

We'll discuss student loan debt in "Key #5—Drop the Debt Weight" and how to save for college in "Key #6—Save in More Ways than One."

Utilities, Cable, Internet, and Other Services

Your utilities, cable, Internet service, and other services can really cost you. Checking these bills regularly will help you stay on top of any rate increases or billing errors.

If you notice a significant spike in a utility bill, take a look at your usage. Is your bill based on an estimated reading? This is usually denoted on your bill. My bill marks it as ACT (actual) or EST (estimate). If it's an estimate, you may want to check your meter yourself and call customer service to have your bill adjusted (if possible).

If it is based on an actual reading and you have a year's worth of records, you may want to compare your usage against the same period last year. Has your usage changed? Or did your utility rates significantly increase? If there was minimal change in your usage and no significant rate increase, this may be worth a phone call to customer service.

Always keep an eye out for price increases. Sometimes cable and Internet providers offer promotional rates that expire. And if you call them, you may be able to take advantage of another promotion or negotiate a lower rate. If not, it may be time to shop around for a better price. In "Key #6—Save in More Ways Than One," I'll share some tips to help you reduce your utility bills.

Medical Bills

As with any other type of bill, be sure to review your medical bills and explanation of benefits (EOB) statements. Understanding how your benefits work will help you save money. For example, if you have 100% coverage on your annual wellness without a copayment requirement, then you should not be paying a $20 copayment for your annual wellness visit.

Hospital bills can be difficult to review, but you should try to review them as best you can. And feel free to reach out to the billing department or your insurance provider for more information. Checking your explanation of benefits statement will help you confirm that you are paying the right amount for your services.

Beware of being double-billed. There have been a few occasions when I noticed billing discrepancies between my medical benefits statement and what I paid the healthcare provider. And in both instances, I notified the provider and received refunds.

Watch the Cash Register

When it comes to shopping, I may be the person who annoys you in the checkout line. I'm a cash register watcher, and I always check to see if the price is right. My mom taught me how to do this well. It requires some effort, but you can really save money and even get some of your purchases free.

Always check to make sure the price you pay is correct. It should match the advertised or displayed price. And depending on the store, you may even receive it free when it's wrong, as some grocery stores offer price guarantees. I've received free chicken, produce, eggs, bread, and many other things. Many price guarantee policies have limits, such as the item must be $6 or less. Familiarize yourself with your store's policy, and you could get free stuff too.

Checking and remembering prices is like anything else in life—the more you do it, the better you get. When I find a price error, I simply tell the sales clerk and he or she orders a price check or looks in the sales ad to verify the price. This has become a habit of mine when I go shopping, so any time I find an error I receive a price adjustment or get it free. If you don't want to be a cash register watcher, then I encourage you to at least review your receipt. You'd be surprised of the types of errors you could find.

Still not convinced? Well, one time I went to a major discount retailer to buy some birthday candles. They happened to be on clearance for only $0.39. However, when the clerk rang them up, they scanned for over $40. I was shocked, as were the sales clerk and other customers in line.

Watching the register and checking your sales receipt can save you money. Besides, who has money to waste on a price error?

Invest Wisely

> *"Never invest in a business you cannot understand."*
> **–Warren Buffett**

When it comes to investment opportunities, beware of scams. Keep in mind that when an investment sounds too good to be true, it usually is. Get-rich-quick and fast money scams are always out there. If you are a wise investor, you will be able to spot the scams and avoid them. The best way to stay abreast of any scams is to listen to your local or national news alerts. You can also find any government-issued warnings on the Federal Trade Commission's website, ftc.gov (Consumer Protection tab).

Investing opportunities may sound very appealing, but it's best to be cautious. Take your time and execute due diligence in evaluating the investment. Due diligence is when you thoroughly research and fully understand the investment before you invest your money.

When you feel pressured to invest now, take a step back and really think about it. The key to identifying scams is to take it slow and evaluate the entire investment fully before taking any action. It may be wise to reach out to someone you know and trust with experience in that particular area to get his or her thoughts on the investment opportunity. If it is an investment that you know right away is one the person would discourage you from investing in, then you already have a red flag indication to walk away from the opportunity.

Warren Buffett is a well-known, respected, and successful investor. According to *Forbes* magazine, he is one of the richest men in the world. His investment strategy is very disciplined and long-term focused. I believe the best way to learn is to learn from the best. So, I'd like to share some of his words of wisdom on investing:

- "Rule No. 1: Never lose money. Rule No. 2: Never forget rule No. 1."
- "You're neither right nor wrong because other people agree with you. You're right because your facts are right and your reasoning is right—and that's the only thing that makes you right. And if your facts and reasoning are right, you don't have to worry about anybody else."
- "Risk comes from not knowing what you're doing."
- "A public-opinion poll is no substitute for thought."
- "You ought to be able to explain why you're taking the job you're taking, why you're making the investment you're making, or whatever it may be. And if it can't stand applying pencil to paper, you'd better think it through some more. And if you can't write an intelligent answer to those questions, don't do it."

To learn more about investing you may want to read *The Intelligent Investor* by Benjamin Graham. When it comes to investing, the golden rules I follow are:

- Understand the investment and any potential risks upfront.
- Don't follow the pack. I remember one time when my colleague went around the office telling everyone to invest in such and such stock. A few weeks later he regretted his investment as he had lost a lot of his money and it was still going down.
- Research the investment and understand the true value.
- Discuss the investment opportunity with someone I consider to have expertise in that specific area.
- Make sure it is a decision my husband and I would be comfortable with in the long run.

Kevin's Story

Kevin was living paycheck to paycheck and needed to increase his cash flow to keep up with his monthly expenses. Someone he knew told him about an incredible investment opportunity that required $25,000 cash to get started. The person wanted Kevin to partner with him to purchase a large amount of merchandise to sell on the Internet. Kevin was sold on the great earning potential (over 200% return) and the sales pitch he received, which seemed very promising and profitable. It sounded like the best investment opportunity ever, but he didn't have enough cash to get started, given that he was already struggling to make ends meet.

Kevin asked his parents to make the investment instead. He convinced them to join in on this huge investment opportunity to grow their money. They took out a home equity loan and withdrew from their retirement savings to come up with the money. Kevin then took the $25,000 in cash to his future business partner to jumpstart the business.

But it was all a scam and never manifested into anything that he was told or sold. It only resulted in a large loss for everyone who put money in. It was devastating, because the man left town and could not be found. Unfortunately, Kevin made the investment without a contract and did not have any documentation to support the large cash investment transaction. He did not even have any tangible transaction proof or the man's real name to file any charges with the police. Needless to say, this was a very expensive learning experience.

The moral of Kevin's story: it's important to spend the time upfront to research and understand any investment. Get a contract agreement in writing before investing in any joint ventures. Also, any investment that has a significant cash-only requirement and requires you to borrow money to invest is a bad sign from the start. If you do not have the money to invest, then it may not be the right timing for you. Because, like Kevin, it could just put you further in debt.

"The ability to say "no" is a tremendous advantage for an investor."
–Warren Buffett

Track Your Money

A friend of mine shared with me her brother's secret to becoming a self-made millionaire. His wife. Yes, this was really her answer. And no, he did not marry an heiress or anything. He did, however, marry someone who believed in tracking the money spent. She was very diligent about writing everything down that they spent their money on. They did this over a number of years and eventually became millionaires.

I am sure this practice was accompanied with wise money habits (spending, saving, and investing). However, she stressed that actively monitoring their expenses accounted for most of their success.

It may be helpful for you to keep a better eye on your expenses if you start to track your money too. Because when you see how much you're spending and on what, it's easier to identify cost-cutting opportunities. You can use personal finance software, online tools (see "Key #4—Live Below Your Means to Get Ahead" for more details on budgeting tools) or manually track your spending using a checkbook register, a spreadsheet entry system, or a notepad. Choose the method that works best for you. This level of tracking will help you watch where your money goes at the most granular level of detail. Who knows? You may become a self-made millionaire too!

Get Started

Organization helps you watch where your money goes. Create a filing system and be diligent about reviewing receipts, bills, statements, and any other documents. Your file system may be as simple as a plastic file bin and some manila folders. Label it by month/year and file your bills and statements after review. This new system of organization will come in handy during tax season.

I realize this is a wealth of information, and it may be a bit overwhelming at first. I'd suggest you get started by taking small steps. Make a list of the top three actions you will start doing to watch where your money goes:

1. _____

2. _____

3. _____

Focus on mastering the areas you've listed. Practicing these methods and paying more attention to details will keep more money in your pocket. Once you have accomplished the top three, start focusing on other areas.

Before long, you'll find yourself having better money habits, and it will just become a part of you. It's just like learning to ride a bike. The thought of learning how to ride may be scary at first, but with persistence and practice, before long you're riding like the wind and beaming with confidence.

Key Summary

- Check your paycheck to make sure you are paid correctly.

- Understand any financial product (costs, terms, details) before you open an account.

- Bank smarter and use credit wisely. Review your account statement to verify your balance, transactions, charges, and account activity.

- Actively monitor and manage your loans to confirm your payments and interest rates.

- Manage your student loan debt effectively and commit to your repayment strategy.

- Check your utilities, cable, Internet, and medical statements to identify any errors or promotions ending and to avoid being overcharged.

- Watch the register or check your sales receipt to make sure the price you pay is correct.

- Invest wisely—watch out for scams, and research and understand your investment upfront.

- Track your money to find out where it goes.

- Get organized!

Key #4

LIVE BELOW YOUR MEANS TO GET AHEAD

"There are plenty of ways to get ahead.
The first is so basic I'm almost embarrassed to say it:
spend less than you earn."
–Paul Clitheroe

Living above your means comes with a heavy price. And the price you pay for this type of lifestyle may far exceed the money it costs you to keep up. When you live above your means, it forces you to live from paycheck to paycheck. Even worse, you may find yourself clinging to credit cards like life support, just to make it from month to month.

Living this type of lifestyle could quickly lead to financial turmoil, and you'd suddenly find yourself drowning in thousands of dollars of credit card debt, with piles of bills and bad credit. But when you look beyond the money, what is the real cost? Could it be YOU? After all, financial burdens can weigh you down with stress and anxiety and negatively impact your quality of life, health, and relationships.

According to the American Psychological Association's 2010 Stress in America[8] survey, money is a leading cause of stress. This isn't very shocking, considering the economy is still recovering from a recession while the costs of food, gas, and other necessities are rising.

When it comes to your spending habits, are you living above, within, or below your means? Here's how I would define each lifestyle:

- **Living above your means.** This is when you spend more money than you make. The money you make includes your take-home pay (income after taxes and any other deductions) plus any other income sources you may have, such as rental income, alimony, interest, dividends, pension, and Social Security.

An example of someone living above his means is Bobby. Bobby earns $3,000 a month, but he spends $3,500 a month on expenses. Because he is spending more than he makes—$500 more— Bobby is living above his means.

You may be questioning how he could possibly spend more money than he makes. The answer: he is probably using savings or credit to make up the difference. If Bobby were using his credit card, he could easily rack up more than $6,000 of credit card debt in a year ($500 per month x 12 months). And that doesn't even include any interest charges. As you can see, people who use their credit cards to cover the gap between income and money spent can quickly find themselves in significant debt.

---

8 American Psychological Association's 2010 Stress in America Report, retrieved from http://www.apa.org/news/press/releases/stress/national-report.pdf

- **Living within your means.** This is when your spending is equal to what you make. While you are living within your means, which is a good thing, you have nothing left to save and are only a paycheck away from living above your means.

- **Living below your means.** This is when you spend less than what you make. For example, Charles makes $4,000 a month and spends only $2,800 of his income every month. Charles is living below his means by $1,200 a month. That amounts to $14,400 a year. What would you do with an extra $14,400 a year? When you spend less than what you make, the choice is yours. You can save and invest for the future, and you can escape living paycheck to paycheck.

So, how are living (above, within, or below)?

If you're living above your means today, you're not alone. There are many people across all income levels that find themselves living paycheck to paycheck, including those making six-figure salaries and even those earning millions. Now that you know where you stand today, you can start working to get where you want to be tomorrow.

Start looking for opportunities to reduce expenses (e.g., eating out), spend less (e.g., coupons, bundles), and increase your income. These changes will make it easier for you to stop living paycheck to paycheck and start saving and investing for a better financial future. Plus, changing your lifestyle will reduce financial stress, anxiety, or any pressure you may be feeling. So you can enjoy life.

If you're living within your means, you are in a good position to start living below your means. Look for areas where you can reduce your expenses and eliminate any wasteful spending (remember to watch where your money goes). Before you know it, you'll be living below your means.

If you're living below your means already, that's great news! I still encourage you to take a look at your expenses to identify any cost-cutting opportunities and to keep a close eye on your spending.

No matter where you stand today, I'll show you how you can manage your money better, spend less, and avoid many of the traps that make you feel like you have to spend more than you make.

Do You Have a Budget?

"Budget: a mathematical confirmation of your suspicions."
–A.A. Latimer

Some people hate to even think of a budget, because it makes them feel limited. However, having a budget helps you take control of your spending. Budgets give you better insight into where your money is going and help you manage your money more effectively to reach your financial goals. Budgets also make it easier for you to be proactive about your finances and to identify cost-cutting opportunities.

If you have a working budget, you can easily tell whether you are living above, within, or below your means. Yes, even if you have a budget it doesn't guarantee you're living below your means. You're still in complete control; a budget just shows you how you're living.

So, what's a working budget? It's a budget that shows your income and spending (actual vs. planned) continually. Your monthly spending includes your normal expenses, such as rent, mortgage, utilities, and groceries, as well as other expenditures such as eating out, gym memberships, clothing, and entertainment. It's a complete picture of where your money is going. Be sure to include any annual expenses. For example, we pay our homeowner's association fee yearly. I simply take the total cost (annual homeowner's association fee) and divide it by twelve to show the monthly cost in our budget.

New technology has definitely made creating budgets easier now than in the past. User-friendly software applications and free online tools are available to create and manage your budget. Some popular personal finance software and online budgeting tools you may want to consider:

- Quicken
- AceMoney
- YNAB (You Need A Budget)
- Mint.com
- Wesabe.com
- Money.Strands.com

While technology makes things easier, you can also create your budget simply using a notepad or spreadsheet.

Here are the steps to create a budget:

1. **Document your total monthly income.** Be sure to list the income amount and source. This includes take-home pay, alimony, child support, rental property income, or any other miscellaneous income (e.g., investments) you might receive every month.
2. **Document your normal monthly expenses.** This list includes expenses such as your mortgage, rent, car payment, insurance, utilities, gym membership, or any other monthly recurring expense.

3. **Document your variable expenses.** These expenses may vary from month to month. Some examples include groceries, eating out, gas, car repair, dry cleaning, gift purchases, and entertainment.

4. **Calculate your overall budget summary:**
   a. Calculate **total monthly expenses** by adding normal monthly expenses and variable monthly expenses.
   b. Calculate **remaining income** by subtracting your total monthly expenses from your total monthly income.

After you create your budget, look for areas in which you can save more and spend less. "Key #6: Save in More Ways Than One" will help you do this.

Below is a budget plan you can use to get started:

MONTHLY INCOME			
Description	**Planned**	**Actual**	**Difference**
Example - Net Pay	$1,500		
Total Income			

NORMAL MONTHLY EXPENSES

Description	Planned	Actual	Difference
Example - Rent	$750		
Total Normal Expenses			

VARIABLE MONTHLY EXPENSES

Description	Planned	Actual	Difference
Example—Gas	$120		
Total Variable Expenses			

Total Income - Total Expenses (Normal + Variable) = Remaining Income

Remaining Income	Planned	Actual	Difference
Total Remaining Income			

By following the steps above, you have created your budget and determined your remaining income. Your remaining income is the amount you have left after paying your monthly expenses. A balanced budget is one that shows your monthly income equal to or greater than your monthly expenses.

This will tell you mathematically whether you are living above, within, or below your means. If your remaining income is negative, you are living above your means. If this is you today, it's OK—because now that you know where you stand, you can change what you're doing (reduce spending, eliminate debt, increase income) to *Get Your Money Right.*

A remaining income of zero indicates that you are living within your means. If this is you, it's good to know that you are living within your means. To start living below your means, again, find areas in which you can reduce your expenses.

A positive remaining income value means that you are already living below your means. Congratulations on this remarkable accomplishment! Please keep in mind there may still be opportunities for you to reduce your spending. Use your remaining income to achieve your financial goals, such as paying off debt or saving for retirement.

Start reviewing and tracking against your budget every month, so you maintain a working budget. Then you can see how you are performing against your planned spending. It will show you what you're doing right and where you need to improve. Be sure to make any adjustments where necessary to align your budget with your goals.

An example of someone's simple spending budget may look like the following:

MONTHLY INCOME

Pay	$2,104.00
Stipend	$580.00
Total Monthly Income	**$2,684.00**

MONTHLY EXPENSES

Mortgage	$515.00
Electricity	$50.00
Home Phone	$22.00
Cell Phone	$54.00
Water & Sewage	$38.00
Credit Card #1	$26.00
Credit Card #2	$34.00
Credit Card #3	$28.00
School Loan	$134.00
Tithe	$180.00
Gas	$140.00
Car Insurance	$60.00
Renter's Insurance	$75.00
Food	$120.00
Salon Services	$95.00
Cable	$46.00
Savings	$120.00
Internet	$24.00
Condo Maintenance Fee	$200.00
Total Monthly Expenses	**$1,961.00**

Remaining Income	**$723.00**

Budgets show you where your money is coming from and where it is going to help you manage it more effectively. You're in complete control of setting, tracking, and sticking to your budget. Managing your budget can give you more peace of mind in personal finance matters.

Why Are People Living Above Their Means?

Sure, it may sound like common sense to *spend less than you earn*. But there are many reasons why people spend more than they earn. I believe some of the biggest reasons are:

- Easier access to credit
- We live in a "now" society that thrives on instant gratification
- Peer pressure
- Keeping up with the Joneses
- Lack of understanding of financial principles
- Less discipline with our spending habits

I'm going to explore these reasons a little more closely and share techniques you can use to avoid these traps in the future. I know many of the decisions we make are based on what we know and are comfortable doing. However, I encourage you to be open for change. I've seen firsthand the positive difference it makes when you understand your behavior, increase your awareness, and take the necessary actions to drive the change you truly desire.

Easier Access to Credit

You reap the benefits when you use credit wisely—pay on time and in full. Or it could cost you big time in high interest charges.

The credit card industry has evolved since it started in the early 1950s. At that time, credit card offers were limited to a select few.

And credit card approval could have required an applicant to be approved for a loan or meet face-to-face with a bank representative. Over time, the credit card industry transformed itself from one in which credit was carefully given into one in which credit is fairly easy to get.

Technology improved the speed of the credit approval process and made it easier for lenders to assess customer risk levels. As a result, in the 1990s lenders expanded the number of customers they targeted for credit cards and extended more credit. Consumers were lured into new credit cards with special introductory rates and other incentives, and the application process was made quick and easy.

I remember my first exposure to credit cards, which happened in the early 1990s in college. It seemed as though credit card companies were very strategic in placing their representatives in the most heavily populated areas on campus. Representatives were all smiles, clipboards in hand, trying to entice you to fill out credit card applications. It looked as though they were practically giving away credit cards. They even offered special gifts to apply, like t-shirts and water bottles.

Anything free gets a college student's attention, especially when all you have to do is fill out a short application. And it worked, because you'd see huddles of students filling out credit card applications and walking away, their free giveaways in hand. And while the free gift was nice, what really grabbed students was the chance to be approved for that credit card. Because being approved meant you had access to "free money" to buy stuff! The reality, of course, was that credit gave you access to borrowed money. The only way it would be free is if you paid your balance in full every month.

As competition among credit card companies intensified, their marketing campaigns got stronger, and the number of households with credit cards grew, as did consumer spending. After all, credit cards provided more purchasing power and made many of us spend more money. In fact, it was reported that 1999 was the first year when we saw U.S. consumer spending exceed earnings. In other words, consumers were using credit cards to spend more than they made. Carrying debt became a way of life.

How Did We Start Spending More Than We Earn?

Is there a mental disconnect between spending cash and charging your purchases? Passing someone a piece of plastic to cover a purchase doesn't seem to have the same effect as when you pay with real money—paper and coins. Studies have shown that people spend more money using credit than cash.

What about those convenience checks? You know, the special checks you might find in your monthly statement or mailbox? Sure, you can use the checks at your convenience, but it's going to cost you. If you read the fine print, you'll find out just how much. I received one of these offers just the other day, and the underlying sales message was to use the check now and pay for it later.

Could the constant "buy now, pay later" philosophy from the credit card companies be the reason we spend more on credit? Or could the real culprit be the cleverly designed minimum payment option? You know, where you have the option to spend $1,400 now and only pay the $40 minimum payment? Credit cards give you the opportunity to spend thousands of dollars now and pay a nominal fee every month. Given this choice, shopping sprees are bound to happen, right? In the short term this may have seemed like a real deal. Besides, many people never really looked beyond the "minimum amount due" box and asked: How much interest is this costing me? How long will it take me to pay the balance?

Thankfully, with the passage of the Credit Card Accountability, Responsibility, and Disclosure Act of 2009, new regulations have provided consumers more disclosure. For example, lenders are required to give you a minimum payment warning on your credit card statement. This shows you an estimate of the time it could take you to pay off your balance and the amount of interest you could pay when you pay only the minimum payment. Now you can see the numbers behind the minimum payment—the years it could take you to pay it off and the cost in interest, which could result in your paying two to three times the original amount borrowed.

Sadly, some people have become addicted to credit and accept debt as a way of life. Someone may ask, "Why save for a new $700 camera when I can charge it and take it home today?" It's that "buy now, pay later" philosophy. Before we know it, we've become comfortable spending more than we earn. But the real cost of this behavior is delivered right to your mailbox. Suddenly we find ourselves in high debt, as purchases keep adding up with finance charges and fees.

What About Home Equity Lines and Loans?

In the early 2000s the housing boom really started taking off, with home values doubling and tripling in some parts of the country. This opened the door for new credit offers and home equity lines and loans. These financial products were less risky for lenders, because your home secured them. These offers were also attractive to homeowners looking for ways to cash out on the equity in their homes to fund home improvements, education costs, new cars, medical expenses, and other things and to pay down high-interest credit cards.

After all, the home equity interest rates were lower than those of personal loans or credit cards. And the interest on home equity lines and loans may even be tax deductible.

Similar to credit cards, home equity lines and loans offered homeowners easier access to credit and more purchasing power.

Personally, when I received home equity offers in the mail, I shredded the applications. I handled them this way because I'm risk averse and try to limit debt, although people were constantly telling me how good of a deal I was passing up.

How to Avoid the Debt Trap

Even though credit may be easy to get, it's important to be disciplined about how you manage your credit. While you may receive attractive credit offers, limit the amount of credit you get to what you actually need.

Start thinking and treating credit like money. And adopt the philosophy of "buy what you can pay for now." Don't fall for those clever marketing tactics that suggest you "buy now, pay later." This will help you minimize the possibility of using credit to supplement your income. In other words, avoid using credit to live above your means.

Credit cards offer you great benefits like cash back, travel insurance, rewards, special discounts, and travel perks. And when you use your credit card responsibly (pay the balance every month, pay on time), you can maximize these benefits. My friend Travis calls them the best "thirty-day interest-free loans."

Sure, there may be times in your life when you're unable to pay your balance in full every month. This happened to me after college when I transitioned into the workforce. During this time I was very cautious about my spending habits and limited myself to charging only what I needed. And when the bill arrived, I paid as much as I could afford. Once my financial situation improved, I quickly returned to my normal practice of paying my balance in full every month to avoid any finance charges.

The "Now" Society

> *"Be assured that it gives much more pain to the mind to be in debt, than to do without any article whatever which we may seem to want."*
> –Thomas Jefferson

When I was growing up in the 70s and early 80s, people believed in delayed gratification. Delayed gratification is when you are willing to wait for something you want. In those days, if you wanted something you couldn't afford to buy, you would save and buy it later. Sure, credit was harder to get, but people still delayed their gratification until they had the money to buy whatever it was they wanted.

This way of life was common, and retailers knew it. That's why they created programs like layaway, where customers could purchase an item over time using a payment plan. After the item had been fully paid for, the customer received it. These payment programs were so popular that stores designated a special area to handle layaway purchases. You'd see people standing in layaway lines, just like you'd see them at the checkout. There wasn't any negative stigma associated with it, and people spoke freely about items they'd put on layaway. Layaway still exists in some stores today. During The Great Recession, it even appeared to be making somewhat of a comeback, as lenders were reducing credit limits.

Another example of how we used to save and plan ahead for our purchases was Christmas savings accounts. Have you ever heard of them? They were special savings accounts you could contribute money to year round. Then, when Christmas arrived, you would have enough money saved up to buy gifts.

In the past, people were more active in planning, budgeting, and saving for the future. Today, our money habits have drastically changed. Perhaps, the "buy now, pay later" credit philosophy has changed the way we spend money and has helped fuel the "now" society we live in today. There is less self-control and more emphasis on instant gratification. Instant gratification comes when you make an impulsive decision to buy something immediately. An impulse purchase is one that is unplanned and happens unexpectedly.

As you reflect on your spending habits, ask yourself: Do you practice delayed gratification? Do you save for large purchases or special occasions? Or are you more inclined just to charge it and worry about paying for it later?

While writing this book, I wondered whether our spending habits are shaped by our generations. Being a Generation Xer myself, I thought it would be helpful to get someone from Generation Y's perspective. I asked her what information would be helpful to Generation Y readers. Her response was very insightful. She said:

Many people in my age group got everything they wanted when they were growing up. Most of us need to learn to live within our means and need to have more financial discipline. When we were most impressionable the economy was doing well and people gave their kids a lot. As a result, our expectations went up and some of us have difficulty in the current economic en-

*vironment, because we are spoiled. We never had any real eco-
nomic crisis in comparison to those who grew up in the Generation X era. Some of us tend to be wasteful, and it is important
that we understand how to live within our means.*

Her perspective was very interesting to me. And to think she used
the words "living within your means" twice. Following our conversation, I conducted some additional research and found she was
right on point with the need for financial literacy. Specifically, one
of Emma Jones' MSN Money articles explained the state of financial
literacy for the younger generation:

> *And yet stats indicate our generation's financial literacy is
> abysmal, with personal finances to match. Only 52% of high
> school seniors passed a recent national financial literacy test,
> meaning adults entering the work force do not know enough
> about basic budgeting, interest rates or taxes to make sound
> decisions for their own lives.*[9]

That article quoted Carmen Wong, author of "Gener@tion Debt:
Take Control of Your Money—A How-To Guide." Wong further said:

> *We're in a generation that was kind of shielded from a lot of
> financial responsibilities. Twenty years ago, when you were in
> college you didn't have a credit card, and (now) all of a sudden
> we had to take on debt to go to college. Then we get out of col-
> lege and we have to have that handbag and an iPod . . . It is so
> easy to take on debt."*[10]

---

9 Johnson, Emma. "Why Generation Y Is Broke," MSN Money. Accessed April 12,
  2011. http://articles.moneycentral.msn.com/Investing/HomeMortgageSavings/
  WhyGenerationYIsBroke.aspx#pageTopAchor.
10 Ibid.

In my experience I've found that financial literacy is needed across all generations. When it comes to reversing the trend of the "now" society, we all have to practice delayed gratification. Besides, waiting is a good thing. You could change your mind about making the purchase or find a better deal elsewhere.

Breaking Away From the "Now" Society

To get away from the "now" society, we must take a step back and ask ourselves this question: Is this something I need or want? And yes, there is a difference.

Merriam-Webster.com defines the words as follows:
- **Need**: to be needful or necessary
- **Want**: to have a strong desire for

For some reason, needs and wants seem to get blurred at times. For purposes of this book, a need is something that is a must-have. On the contrary, a want is something nice to have but unnecessary. The table below shows the difference between needs and wants:

NEED	WANT
a place to live	a penthouse in New York
food to eat	dinner at the new steakhouse downtown
clothes to wear	a certain name brand of clothes
eyeglasses to see	colored contacts
hearing aid to hear	ears pierced
time away	extravagant vacation

When you prioritize your needs over wants, you are able to control your spending. You're waking up your money consciousness and asking, "Do I really need this?" before making purchases. This awareness helps you make better financial decisions and live below your means.

The easiest way to break away from the "now" society is to practice delayed gratification and prioritize your needs over wants. When you do this well, you'll notice the positive difference it makes in your bank account.

Standing Your Ground, Despite the Pressure

"You can't base your life on other people's expectations."
–Stevie Wonder

Peer pressure has the ability to impact our lives in many ways. You may remember a class bully who forced you to give him your lunch money, but peer pressure doesn't necessarily end in school. If we let it, peer pressure could impact us our entire lives.

Dictionary.com defines peer pressure as: "social pressure by members of one's peer group to take a certain action, adopt certain values, or otherwise conform in order to be accepted."[11]

Financial peer pressure happens when we let the thoughts, opinions, comments, and expectations of others influence our buying decisions. Be it right or wrong, one person's simple comment may cause another to feel as though he has to buy a bigger home than he can afford just to be accepted.

---

11 Dictionary.com. Accessed April 12, 2011.
   http://dictionary.reference.com/browse/peer+pressure Unabridged
   Based on the Random House Dictionary, © Random House, Inc. 2011.

A friend of mine feels particularly strong about the role peer pressure plays in personal finance, and she encouraged me to include her personal story in my book. She's the wife of a former professional athlete, and she told me how people had certain expectations for what she should own and wear. For example, people told her the type of car she should drive and the brand of handbag she should carry. The best part of her ordeal is that she didn't let their opinions influence her buying decisions, because she didn't give in to them.

She and her husband were confident about making their own financial decisions independently. They chose to live in a nice, comfortable home over the million-dollar homes the other athletes may have lived in. As a result of their combined efforts, they are both still doing well, long after his sports career has ended.

Yes, peer pressure is real. But we still have the power to make our own decisions. After all, we're the ones who have to pay for the types of lifestyles we choose to live.

People will always have their opinions. However, we must be careful not to let their thoughts and expectations influence our spending habits. If you have a certain type of job or earn a high income, there will always be those people who feel the need to tell you that you should be doing this or that with your money. But remember, it's your money, so you can do with it as you please.

> *"I don't know the key to success, but the key to failure is trying to please everybody."*
> —**Bill Cosby**

I remember back when I was a manager and a colleague offered to drive me to my car after a late night at work. I gladly took him up on his offer, given the fact that my car was parked far away. He kindly drove me in his nice, luxurious Audi sports car. When we pulled up to my car, a look of surprise came over his face.

You see, we were both executives, but instead of a luxurious car I drove a nice and well-maintained Nissan Maxima. It was the same car I had purchased a few years after I joined the company, but it was nearly four years old at the time.

He could not believe that was my car. Finally he asked, "Is that really your car?"

I answered, "Yes."

He proceeded to tell me in a very matter-of-fact tone, "Well, you're an executive and you should have a better car."

I kindly replied, "When I bought my car, I said that I would keep it for ten years. And executive or not, that is what I plan to do."

He just shook his head in disbelief and smiled in complete amazement. I didn't let what he said offend me, because he was just expressing the way he felt. Besides, there were entry-level people working at our company who drove "better" cars than I did. They may have driven Lexuses (that came with larger car payments), but I was content to have my car (at a fraction of the cost). Besides, it was a Nissan Maxima SE Limited, to be exact. And I was confident as ever, because I knew things like my car don't define me. Only I can define me.

Nevertheless, I could have been offended by his words and spent the entire evening crying my eyes out. And I could have opted to trade in my car for a luxury model to be more accepted. But no, I couldn't do it, because I can only be me.

The truth is, luxury car or not, we were both still executives working for the same company. The only real difference is that I was probably pocketing more of my salary driving the less expensive car without a car payment. I say you've got to just stand your ground, despite the pressure.

Sometimes we look for things to validate us. But if you know who you are, you don't need things to be accepted. Dare to be different. When you're comfortable thinking and acting differently, you'll be happier and have more in the long run anyway.

Divas Live Below Their Means Too . . .

Beyoncé Knowles is a famous multitalented celebrity worth millions of dollars. In 2010, Beyoncé was listed as one of *Forbes'* top ten earning celebrities. Yet this diva knows the importance of living below her means. In fact, she happens to be quite frugal. A frugal person is one who is careful in how he or she spends money.

> Beyoncé revealed her frugal spending habits to *The Mirror*:
> *"Honestly, I'm very frugal. I haven't bought a car since I was 16 or any diamonds since I was 17. I have a lot of property. I've invested my money and I don't have to make any more, thank God, because I'm set," Beyoncé, 27, told The Mirror.*
>
> She adds, *"I'm now able to really be free and just do things that make me happy. It's an effort to stay grounded."*[12]

---

12 By permission from The Mirror. http://www.mirror.co.uk/celebs/latest/2009/02/20/
beyonce-i-am-very-frugal-115875-21139339/

Can you believe Beyoncé's frugal? She is taking control of her money and planning for tomorrow. And she's happy to be living that way instead of paycheck to paycheck. I highly doubt she'll be one of those stars forced to file for bankruptcy after squandering away millions.

"They Live Well Below Their Means."
–The Millionaire Next Door [13]

I think we have all been there with peer pressure. Always remember that things don't define you—only you can! You have to stand your ground and be confident about who you are. Besides, what you think about yourself speaks louder than any famous designer handbag or outfit ever would. It's your money, so shouldn't you be the one who decides how to spend it?

Live Your Life and Forget About the Joneses

"Too many people spend money they haven't earned, to buy things they don't want, to impress people they don't like."
–Will Smith

While peer pressure is fueled by outward forces, "keeping up with the Joneses" is of our own doing. People are said to be keeping up with the Joneses when they compare what they have to what other people have and try to compete by buying the same things to maintain their social status. For example, if your neighbor buys new furniture, you suddenly feel the urge to buy furniture too. Whether it's your neighbor or someone else, people are said to be keeping up with the Joneses when they base their purchasing decisions on those of others.

---

13 Stanley, Thomas J. and William D. Danko. *The Millionaire Next Door* (New York: Pocket, 1999), 27.

Commercials often poke fun at the idea of keeping up with the Joneses. I remember one commercial that showed two neighbors living across the street from each other. One neighbor drives home with a brand new car. The other neighbor peers out the window and calls to his wife, saying, "It's time to buy a new car."

Some people feel the need to buy things just to keep up with the family across the street, and this type of spending behavior normally stems from status, self-esteem, or image. The Joneses could signify anyone in your life, such as family members, friends, or coworkers.

The destructive thing about this behavior is that some people do this regardless of their financial situations, which causes them to live above their means. When it comes to keeping up with the Joneses, I encourage you to forget about the Joneses and live your own life.

Comparing what we have to others leads to unhappiness and in some cases poor financial decisions. We are all running our own race, and you are in control of your own destiny. So lead yourself down the right path by pursuing your vision and achieving your own personal goals. If you're distracted by what others have, you could get off course. Remember, dare to be different.

Improve Your Financial Understanding

"Formal education will make you a living;
self-education will make you a fortune."
–Jim Rohn

I learned the importance of understanding personal finance at a very young age. And today I still spend countless hours to gain additional knowledge in a financial industry that is constantly changing.

Why? Because I've found that when it comes to money, what you don't know can cost you!

Education is a critical component of our personal development. As you read this book, remember how fortunate you are to be able to understand the words on this page and obtain knowledge. Think about how much you may have missed out on in life if you couldn't read. How different would your life be? Reading may be something we take for granted, but when you take a moment to think about how different your life would be if you were illiterate, it makes you appreciate it more.

It's also important to be financially literate. A person who is financially literate has the capacity to understand financial concepts independently. Understanding financial concepts makes it easier for you to effectively manage your money and make more informed financial decisions. You're also less likely to be taken advantage of during financial transactions. In other words, people who know more tend to pay less and maximize the benefits of their money. Without financial knowledge, you could be overpaying for financial products, goods, and services.

This book focuses on the fundamentals of personal finance, but there are many financial books that can help you build your knowledge in different areas (e.g., retirement planning, investments). I encourage you to expand your knowledge by reading financial books, magazines, and blogs. GainMoneyControl.com is my personal finance blog, and it includes articles to help you save money, improve your credit, avoid financial pitfalls, and more.

Finding a mentor with strong money management skills or a financial coach is another way you can improve your financial knowledge. Also, attending financial seminars or workshops is a great way to learn more about personal finance. You can even tune in to financial programs to stay up to date on financial news.

A few informative personal finance websites you may want to check out are:
- MyMoney.gov—personal finance basics
- Yahoo.Finance.com—news, stocks, tools, how-to guides
- Kiplinger.com—news, tools, basic financial concepts, reviews
- SmartMoney.com—news, videos, and personal finance advice

Be a Disciplined Spender

"Never spend your money before you have it."
–Thomas Jefferson

Discipline is one of the most important skills in money management. It's what separates those who have money today from those who will have it tomorrow. While many people believe the answer to financial problems is more money, the wise ones know that if you manage what you have well today, you'll have more tomorrow.

Are you a disciplined spender? Ask yourself the following questions:
- Are you more likely to go shopping without a list than with one?
- Do you make impulse purchases?
- Are you weak for advertisements, telemarketers, or end-of-the aisle sale offers?

If you answered yes to any of those questions, then it's time to wake up the disciplined spender in you, because it will help you live below your means and build wealth. Discipline is a common trait found in successful millionaires and billionaires. In the book *The Millionaire Mind,* Thomas Stanley describes millionaires' discipline:

> *A disciplined person sets his or her sights on a lofty target, then figures out productive ways to reach the target. Disciplined people are not easily sidetracked—they could live in a warehouse filled with top-brand alcoholic beverages and not indulge themselves. They could live in a French bakery and not gain weight. Or they could encounter hundreds of economic opportunities and then select the one or two that are best suited to their strengths and the market's needs.* [14]

I remember watching an episode of *The Oprah Winfrey Show* called "Simplify Your Life." On this show they helped people learn to live on less. One guest caught my attention, because she was spending $400 a week on groceries for herself and two sons. And what made this amount even more shocking was the fact that she also spent money eating out. During the show, they uncovered the real reason behind her spending habits was that she was trying to fill the void she had after losing her husband. So they helped her learn how to live on less. She started using a shopping list and bought only what she needed. This simple change drastically improved her shopping experience. It also saved her time and money. Her grocery bill went from hundreds of dollars in one shopping trip to under $50. [15]

It's true that we may spend money on things to cover up how we feel inside. But when we become disciplined spenders, we are able to understand this and find other solutions to help us break the habit,

---

14 Stanley, Thomas. *The Millionaire Mind* (Kansas City, MO: Andrews McMeel, 2000), 83.
15 Oprah Winfrey's website, accessed April 17, 2011. http://www.oprah.com/slideshow/oprahshow/20090130_tows_livewithout/3.

such as using shopping lists and sticking to budgets. This helps us control our spending better.

Avoid Impulse Purchases

Have you ever noticed when you're ready to check out, there are items placed in your path to entice you to buy more stuff? As you wait to be rung up, they're staring you in the face. If they could talk, they'd be saying, "Buy me." Welcome to the world of impulse purchases, composed of anything and everything to catch your eye. Sure, they may be irresistible, but you're in control—just say no! After all, if you didn't come into the store needing it, how important could it be?

As a mother of two, I dislike checkout lanes the most. My daughters are always picking up items conveniently placed within their reach and asking me, "Mommy, may I have this?" While this is a great teaching opportunity, and I respond, "No, we don't need that," very pleasantly, I could do without the sad face in return. It's not a desirable experience, but I know it will teach them what they need to know as adults to resist those impulse purchases.

Disciplined spenders practice restraint. They shop with purpose and rarely make impulse purchases. Discipline may be hard at first, but you'll get better with practice. Prioritizing needs over wants helps you be more disciplined. As you can see throughout this key, practicing discipline and self-control helps you avoid all the traps and live below your means.

"If you will live like no one else,
later you can live like no one else."
—**Dave Ramsey**

Key Summary

- Spend less than you make.

- Create a working budget, and use your budget to take control of your spending and achieve your financial goals.

- Use credit wisely and avoid the debt trap.

- Practice delayed gratification and prioritize your needs over wants.

- Don't give in to peer pressure. Always remember you—not things—define you.

- Run your own race, and don't be distracted by other people's buying decisions.

- Build on your personal finance knowledge so you can make more informed decisions.

- Be a disciplined spender and watch out for those impulse purchases.

Key #5

DROP THE DEBT WEIGHT

"Our goals can only be reached through a vehicle of a plan, in which we must fervently believe, and upon which we must vigorously act. There is no other route to success."
–Stephen A. Brennan

The burden of debt can really weigh you down. Debt can negatively impact your quality of life with stress and sleepless nights.

You probably know what I mean if your debt is weighing you down. Perhaps the feeling of being overwhelmed only arises at certain times, like when you check the mail. I remember watching the anxiety on Fred G. Sanford's face when he checked his mailbox. Sanford (played by the late Redd Foxx) was the main character in the popular 1970s sitcom *Sanford and Son*. A common theme of the show was how he handled his bills. He was always reluctant to check his mailbox, because all he found inside were bills that he couldn't pay. So he would either toss them in a drawer unopened or just leave them in the mailbox. But it didn't matter what he did, because the bills kept coming back. As Benjamin Franklin once said, "Creditors have better memories than debtors."

Are you feeling overwhelmed by your debt? You may feel pressure when you answer the phone and hear the bill collector's voice. Or you may use your caller ID (what a great invention!) to avoid such calls entirely. Although you don't answer the phone, deep down inside you still feel the pressure over what you owe.

Debt can weigh you down emotionally, with feelings of frustration, anxiety, confusion, stress, fear, anger, and helplessness. If you're burdened by debt, it's time to drop the debt weight so you can start living better. This chapter will show you how to drop the debt weight and lift yourself up again.

Before we get started, there are a few financial terms you should familiarize yourself with: asset, debt, and liability.

Merriam-Webster.com defines these terms as follows:
- asset: an item of value owned
- debt: something owed: obligation
- liability: something for which one is liable

Basically, an asset is something you own that can be converted into cash easily. Examples of assets may include savings, jewelry, stock, real estate, and cars.

Let's focus on debt from a monetary perspective. A debt is something you owe money on to fulfill an obligation. Examples of debt are loans, credit cards, and credit lines. Your debt also includes any IOUs or personal loans; you may have borrowed money from another person such as a family member or friend. A debt is simply anything that you commit (written or orally) to pay back and that has an outstanding balance.

It's been said that there are two kinds of debt—good and the bad. The difference:

- Good debt is acquired when you borrow money to pay for something that is too expensive to pay for in cash that fulfills a need and has long-term value. Some examples of good debt are:
  - Taking out a student loan for a college education, which is an investment in your future
  - Securing a mortgage to purchase an affordable home
  - Acquiring cash to support the start-up costs of a new business venture that would deliver a long-term positive return on investment

- Bad debt is when we borrow money to fund our wants or use it to support our living-above-our-means lifestyle—for instance, going on an extravagant vacation.

A liability, financially speaking, is your obligation to pay money for debt owed. For example, when you take out a mortgage on your home you are liable to pay your monthly payment.

Now's a good time to introduce the concept of net worth. You calculate your net worth by subtracting your total liabilities from your total assets. Your assets might include cash, retirement accounts, savings, and any other valuable possessions that can be converted into cash, such as real estate and jewelry. Examples of liabilities are student loans, credit cards, mortgage, and any other debts owed. Your net worth shows your financial health today. If your liabilities exceed your assets, then you have a negative net worth.

It's been said that your net worth does not equal your self worth. And that's important to know. Whether your net worth is positive or negative, you can increase it by reducing your liabilities (what you owe—*debt weight*) and increasing your assets (what you own).

Three Big Reasons to Drop the Debt Weight

Buying on credit may be easy to do, but we must keep in mind that it is still money that we are obligated to pay back. If you don't pay your debt it could cost you more than the money you owe:

- **Credit score**—Debt may negatively impact your credit score, making it harder for you to be approved or costing you more money in interest and fees.
- **Relationships**—The way we manage our finances has the potential to ruin our friendships and families.
- **Quality of life**—The burden of debt could lead to stress and negatively impact your well-being and health.

Your Credit Matters

> *"The most important thing for a young man is to establish credit—a reputation and character."*
> –John D. Rockefeller

Your credit score is a three-digit number that makes a big difference. It measures your creditworthiness. Businesses and lenders use your credit score to assess your financial risk level. Your credit score helps them determine how likely you will be to pay your bills.

Before you lend somebody money, you would probably consider whether you would be paid back. For example, your friend asks you to lend her $1,000. Before you make your decision, you would probably think about any experiences you've had lending her money. If she always borrows money and never pays you back, then more than likely the answer would be an easy no.

Similarly, lenders use your credit score to make lending decisions based on your history. A FICO score is the most common credit score. FICO is an abbreviation for Fair Isaac Corporation, the company that developed the FICO credit score model. Your FICO score ranges from 300 to 850. The higher your score, the less risk you are to the lender. A lower score signifies more risk and poor creditworthiness, so it's best to aim for a credit score of 700 or higher. A higher credit score saves you money in interest and makes credit approval easier.

You may request your credit score for a fee from one of the three credit bureaus responsible for calculating it. In the United States, your credit rating is calculated by:

- Equifax (www.equifax.com)
- Experion (www.experion.com)
- TransUnion (www.transunion.com)

There are various other websites that also provide your credit score for a fee. A cheaper way to get your credit score is to ask for it when someone pulls your credit report. In the past, I've found lenders who have given me my credit score for free.

Your credit score will probably be different across the credit bureaus, because bureaus use their own calculation formulas, which are kept private. Whatever formula is used, the purpose is the same—to determine a borrower's credit worthiness to a highly accurate degree.

Credit scores give lenders an objective way to evaluate borrowers for mortgages, loans, and credit cards. Your credit report reveals payment history and other relevant credit information. Lenders use it to determine whether you are likely to default on a loan. A loan default is when you do not honor your payment obligation. A person with a higher FICO score is more likely to pay back the loan and is therefore less of a risk. These borrowers receive easier approvals and lower costs (interest rates, fees).

The Fair Isaac Corporation shows you what's in your FICO credit score. The following figure illustrates the factors used in the calculation.[16]

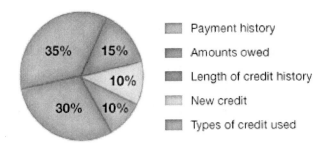

Collectively, these factors help determine your level of credit worthiness.

- **Payment history** (35 percent)—Are you making payments on time? It's important to pay on time, because, as you can see, your payment history is the largest component in determining your FICO score.

---

16 This information is provided by Fair Isaac Corporation, and is used with permission. Copyright ©2001-2011 Fair Isaac Corporation. All rights reserved. FICO is a trademark of Fair Isaac Corporation. Further use, reproduction, or distribution is governed by the FICO Copyright Usage Requirements, which can be found at www.fico.com.

- **Amounts owed** (30 percent)—This is also known as the credit-to-debt ratio. It shows the amount of debt owed compared to the credit available. Ideally, you want to limit your credit use to 50% or less. The lower the amount owed, the better it looks on your credit report. For example, if you have a credit card with a credit limit of $1,000, your outstanding balance should be $500 or less. How are you doing with this now? Have you maxed out any credit cards? Paying down your balances will help you improve your FICO score.

- **Length of credit history** (15 percent)—The length of your credit history provides more information on your creditworthiness.

- **New credit** (10 percent)—How often have lenders and businesses pulled your credit report to open a new account? This is called a credit inquiry, and there are two types: those that impact your credit score and those that do not. New inquiries pulled at your request for credit applications may negatively impact your credit score, because shopping for new credit may be viewed as high risk.

 TIPS

- *Too many new credit inquires could negatively impact your credit score, so limit the number of new credit applications you submit. And be cautious about allowing people to pull your credit report unnecessarily.*

- *You can opt out of prescreening credit offers online at www.optout-prescreen.com. To opt out by phone, call 888-5-OPT-OUT (888-567-8688).*

- **Types of credit used** (10 percent)—Do you have credit cards, auto loans, or mortgages? Creditors look at the types of credit accounts you have outstanding.

To learn more about your FICO score, visit www.myfico.com/crediteducation.

Check Your Credit Report

When is the last time you checked your credit report? Did you know you're entitled to receive a free copy of your credit report every year? The Fair Credit Reporting Act legally requires the three nationwide credit bureaus (Equifax, Experian, and TransUnion) to provide you with a free copy of your credit report every twelve months.

I strongly encourage you to take advantage of this, because it makes it easier for you to actively manage your credit and verify the information being reported. Plus, reviewing your credit report lets you know what you need to work on to improve your credit. You can also identify and resolve any errors, discrepancies, or fraudulent activity, such as identity theft.

Identity theft could be your worst nightmare. It happens when someone uses your personal information to open new accounts or make unauthorized charges. A few years ago, I read about a case in which someone secured a mortgage for more than $400,000 in someone else's name. The earlier you spot identity theft, the better.

To receive your free credit report you can request it online at AnnualCreditReport.com. This site offers additional products and services for a fee. Just say no to the additional offers and receive your free credit report. You can also call 877-322-8228.

It's a quick and easy process to get your credit report online. I received a free copy of mine in less than five minutes. Beware of other websites that try to lure you in with free credit reports, because most of these sites just try to sell you other products and monitoring services. Your annual credit report should be absolutely FREE.

TIP

Monitor your credit report free year round by requesting from a different credit bureau every four months. Basically, you could request your free credit report from Equifax in January, then Experian in May, and TransUnion in September.

When you receive your credit report, check for any errors. Is your personal information (e.g., name, address, Social Security number) correct? Review your account information—balances, account status, and payment history. Your payment history is a big component in determining your credit score. If you're paying your bills on time, does your credit report show it?

If you find any errors that need to be corrected, bring them to the credit bureau's attention. Be sure to follow the credit bureau's process for filing a dispute and include as much information as possible. The instructions for filing a dispute are available on each bureau's website. After that, contact the reporting company to explain the problem.

Your credit matters—the history you build today impacts your tomorrow. So work to build a good credit score. When you have a good credit score you can:

- **Receive easier approval on loans, mortgages, credit cards, and other products or services that require your credit score.**
- **Pay lower interest rates**. For example, a person with a poor credit score may be approved for an auto loan with a 25% interest rate, while someone with good credit is able to take advantage of a 0% interest rate offer at the same dealership.
- **Get deposits waived.** Utilities usually pull your credit report to understand your creditworthiness. If you have good credit, the deposit is often waived, while a person with a lower credit score must pay a deposit to activate his or her account.

- **Pay less for products and services.** Companies may review your credit to qualify you for special offers or to set prices on their services. For example, people with good credit could receive lower insurance premiums.
- **Improve your chances of getting a new job.** Some employers use your credit report to evaluate you for a job. Your good credit score could give you an edge over other qualified candidates.

Debt Impacts Relationships

"Before borrowing money from a friend, decide which you need most."
–American proverb

Financial problems could strain your personal relationships. Money has caused family feuds and destroyed friendships completely. Marriages have even ended over money problems.

Vanessa's Story

Vanessa was full of excitement, especially because she was officially engaged to the most amazing man ever. They were both working hard to plan their wedding, and they had completed all of their premarital counseling sessions. The little time they had available outside of working and wedding planning was spent looking for their new home. Vanessa had already received a preapproval on a mortgage by herself, but she was interested in learning how much more they'd qualify for together.

One morning, on the way to work, Vanessa asked her fiancé for his Social Security number. She needed to provide the mortgage lender with his information so they could find out how much money they would qualify for together.

Initially, he was a bit hesitant to give it to her. Vanessa figured his hesitation was because of the private nature of a Social Security number. Eventually, he wrote it down for her, thinking she would never be able to use it anyway without his presence.

Vanessa couldn't wait to hear their new approval amount and called the lender later that morning. To her surprise, within a very short time, the lender called her back to deliver some very disappointing news. The lender told her that if she added her soon-to-be husband, they would not be approved for a mortgage. Period. She found this news quite alarming because she had always been financially responsible, with credit scores in the 700s. How could it be that together they qualified for nothing? The lender said he felt very sorry for Vanessa. She pressed him for her fiancé's credit score until the lender told her. Vanessa gasped in disbelief at the low score and begged the lender to send her the credit report so that she could work with her fiancé to improve his credit. Reluctantly, the lender forwarded Vanessa her fiancé's credit report.

When Vanessa received it, she spent hours going through it line by line, highlighting and making notes on how they would fix it. And it was difficult, because inside she felt betrayed by her fiancé's lack of openness regarding his finances, and she even contemplated calling off the wedding. In the end, Vanessa discussed the matter with her fiancé and they worked together to get his score up. In less than a year, their hard work paid off because they were finally approved for their mortgage.

Fortunately, Vanessa's story had a happy ending. Her story highlights the importance of being open and honest about your finances with your significant other. If you need help, ask for it and work together to turn things around.

Speaking of relationships, the best advice someone gave me on marriage was "Whatever someone does when you are dating that irritates you, magnify it by a hundred times and decide whether you can live with it." She was going through a divorce at the time and realized that when you are dating, people are usually on their best behavior. So if you have any concerns, take a closer look before you get married. I'm sure Vanessa must have noticed some signs beforehand that she could have acted on. When you're in a relationship, take time to observe your partner's spending habits and money management skills. Is your mate living above his or her means or drowning in debt? If it's the latter, what is he or she doing about it?

Avoid Cosigning for Someone on a Loan

> "A person who can't pay gets another person who
> can't pay to guarantee that he can pay."
> **–Charles Dickens**

I strongly discourage you from cosigning on a loan for someone. When you cosign, you essentially agree to be held accountable for the loan. And depending on the loan's terms, you may be held equally responsible for the loan. Plus, the outstanding debt (amount owed) factors into your credit score.

Further, when you cosign for someone—just like when you lend money to someone—and the person does not pay, it could harm your relationship in addition to negatively impacting your credit score. That's why it's best to avoid cosigning for someone on a loan. Besides, if someone requires a cosigner, he or she must not be creditworthy.

If you're still considering cosigning despite the risks involved—getting stuck making the payments to protect your credit or seeing your credit get ruined—then consider the following to help you make your decision:

- Are you willing to be held accountable for the payment for the term of the agreement? Remember, any late or missed payments show up on your credit report too. This level of responsibility comes with cosigning on a loan.

- Do you have any past payment history that you can use before making this important decision?

- How long have you known the other person? Have you had enough time to evaluate his or her character? It's always surprising to watch those small claims court cases on TV, when someone is trying to recoup the money lent to someone he or she barely knew. Don't let that be you.

- If the other person has a short credit history, perhaps you can use his or her character as a deciding factor. Is he reliable? Does she follow through on her word? When I bought my first car, I could not qualify for the loan because I didn't have enough credit history. Fortunately, my uncle agreed to cosign for me. I appreciated his kindness, and I made all of my payments ahead of time. After six months, I managed to build enough credit history to refinance my car on my own for less.

If you decide to cosign, keep up to date with the status of the loan and review your credit report to verify payments are made on time.

Living up to your personal loans and obligations promotes stronger relationships. A friend told me recently that he was curious about how his best friend from college was doing. I asked him how they lost touch, and he said his best friend never spoke to him after leaving him with a phone bill of more than $1,000 to pay. It's a pity

GET YOUR MONEY RIGHT

that money came between them. I hope you don't let money come between you and the people in your life.

Quality of Life

> *"Will not your debtors suddenly arise?*
> *Will they not wake up and make you tremble?*
> *Then you will become their victim."*
> **–Habakkuk 2:7 (NIV)**

Debt can impact your quality of life. There are many people who are so worried about their finances that they have problems sleeping at night. If you find yourself worrying too much about your debt, Dale Carnegie's book *How to Stop Worrying and Start Living* reveals strategies you can use to become worry-free.

If you're in debt now, then you probably know the negative effects it can have on you—stress, anxiety, fear, pressure. So let's just move forward. Instead of dwelling on it, choose to think positive and be hopeful. Remember to keep the right mindset. Better yet, start visualizing yourself debt-free. Imagine that!

> *"If only the people who worry about their liabilities would think*
> *about the riches they do possess, they would stop worrying."*
> **–Dale Carnegie**

It's Time to Drop the Debt Weight

"Create a definite plan for carrying out your desire, and begin at once, whether you're ready or not, to put it into action."
–Napoleon Hill

Imagine how different your life would be without any debt. Take a few moments and think about it.

What you just thought about is within your reach; all you have to do is drop the debt weight to get it. I know that getting into debt didn't happen overnight, and becoming debt free is going to require your commitment (make the decision), determination (be persistent), and effort (lay out a plan and take action) to turn it around. And yes, you can do it!

Here are some strategies and steps to help you eliminate debt:

1. **Create a debt-free action plan.** Your debt-free action plan includes a list of all of your outstanding debt. If you're using personal finance software, it may have this capability. Or you can simply create your own using a spreadsheet or notepad. Your debt action plan needs to include:
   - **Creditors' information:** List the name of each company or person owed. The easiest way to get started is to use your monthly billing statements and credit report. Be sure to use the most accurate information available.
   - **Interest rate:** This is the current interest rate you are paying on the outstanding balance.
   - **Outstanding balance:** This is the amount owed on the account.

- **Current balance:** Track your current balance every month. Watching your balances drop will motivate you to keep it up!
- **Monthly payment:** This is the amount you pay on your account every month.
- **Credit limit:** This is the credit available on account.
- **Notes:** Document any important account details, such as your account payment strategy, which we'll discuss next. Also include any important account information, such as a special 0% interest rate that expires in six months.

2. **Develop a payoff strategy.** I recommend starting with the highest-interest-rate debt first, because it costs you the most money. However, if you need a sense of accomplishment to stay motivated, then you may decide to start with your lowest account balance first. Choose the payoff strategy that works best for you.

3. **Update your budget and debt-free action plan with your payoff strategy.** Then, look for cost cutting ways to find the extra cash to pay off your debt.

4. **Pay off your first target account and pay the minimum payment on all of your other bills to keep them paid on time.** Apply all extra money toward paying off the first account. After you pay off your first account, continue using your payoff strategy on the remaining accounts. For example, after you pay off credit card X, you have an extra $75 to pay down your next targeted account.

 TIP

As you pay off each account, take time and celebrate your successes. You can do something simple like enjoy your favorite dessert. It does not have to be elaborate, but do something simple to celebrate it. You deserve it!

5. **Negotiate a lower credit card interest rate.** When you're trying to pay off debt, a lower interest rate could save you hundreds or thousands of dollars. The best way to negotiate your interest rate is to gather any credit card offers you have received and use them to come up with your target interest rate. It may be something like 9%. For additional leverage when negotiating, you could use the number of years you have been a customer, past payment history (if you've paid on time), and your credit score (if it's good).

   After you have everything together, call the number on the back of your card and speak with customer service. Be confident and polite and stress your desire to stay with them, but tell them you need a lower (competitive) interest rate. Be sure to use your leverage speaking points (e.g., the number of years you've been a customer) and ask for your target interest rate. If they are unable to give you your target interest rate, ask what the best is that they can do for you. Ask for a supervisor if the representative can't lower your interest rate. If it doesn't work the first time, try again in a week and again in a month. If you keep trying, you may speak with someone who can help you.

6. **Increase your income, sell your stuff, or use cash windfalls to pay down your debt.** You can take on a part-time job, look for a higher paying job, or start getting paid for your hobby to increase your income. For instance, a teacher may consider tutoring after school. Do you have valuables you're not using? Like a single gold hoop earring without a match? Instead of letting it sit in your jewelry box, you could sell it to a gold broker for some cash. Garage sales and websites like eBay and Craigslist are great ways to turn unused items into cash. Also, use cash windfalls, such as a company bonus, to pay down debt.

7. **Should you transfer your credit card balance?** This is a decision you need to make based on the balance transfer options available, your payoff strategy, and the cost. For example, if you're offered a promotional rate of 0% for a year or two, it may be worth your time. Before you decide, review the terms and read the fine print, so you fully understand the transfer offer. A few things to consider: How much does it cost to transfer your balance? When does the low interest rate expire? What is the interest rate after it expires? Do you have the credit available to transfer your balance?

 TIP

Avoid consolidating unsecured credit card debt into home equity lines or loans, because if you cannot pay, you could lose your home.

If you decide transferring your balance is the right choice, here are some tips:
- Pay your bills on time and keep your balance under the credit limit to avoid fees or interest rate hikes.
- Check your statement to verify transfer charges and the interest rate.
- Be disciplined. The goal is to reduce your debt, so make it a practice to only buy what you can afford to pay off at the end of the month on your other card.

8. **Pay off your loan early.** Paying your loan off early saves you money. You can accomplish this by paying more on your principal. Make biweekly payments, in which you pay half of your payment every two weeks. Check with your lender to see if they can handle biweekly payments. Be sure to do it yourself, because lenders will often charge processing fees to put you on their biweekly payment plans.

9. **Refinance your installment loan.** If you can receive a better interest rate on an installment loan elsewhere, you might consider refinancing. For example, if you're paying 11% in interest, you might be able to get a new loan at 5% interest for the same term remaining or less. As with any financial decision, be sure to understand the terms (e.g., payment period) and costs involved to make the right decision. Back in college I saved an extra $40 a month when I refinanced my car. Refinance savings can really add up and help you pay down other debt.

10. **Pay off your mortgage earlier.** Your mortgage is probably your biggest debt. Some tips to help you save money and take years off your mortgage:

- **Make biweekly mortgage payments to get an extra mortgage payment in every year**. Pay half of your loan amount every two weeks. Set the automatic payment up with your financial institution to avoid any setup fees with your lender by doing it yourself.
- **Pay extra (amount you can afford) every month**. This allows you to pay more against the principal amount, which reduces your interest amount over the loan.
- **Make lump sum additional payments on your mortgage.** Apply windfall cash toward your principal. This may include bonuses or tax refunds.
- **Refinance your mortgage for a lower interest rate and shorter repayment term.** If you can receive a low fixed interest rate, then it may be worth refinancing your loan. However, you must consider the cost and benefits. Be cautious about refinancing and extending the term of your loan. After all, the goal is to reduce debt and extending your term could cost you more over the term of the mortgage. Use

mortgage calculators online to help you weigh the costs and benefits upfront. Mortgage calculators take into account different factors such as closing costs and the time you expect to stay in the home. You can find them at Bankrate. com, TheStreet.com, and DaveRamsey.com.

 TIPS:
- *Be sure to check if you have a prepayment penalty. Prepayment penalties may not allow you to pay off your mortgage early or may cost you money.*
- *When considering refinancing a mortgage, remember the goal is to drop the debt weight, so avoid cashing out on equity. Be credit wise.*

11. **Reduce your student loan interest rate or get loan forgiveness.** You may qualify to have your student loan interest rate reduced. Another option is to consolidate your loans. Before you consolidate your loans, be sure to understand the terms of the loan consolidation (lower interest rate, repayment period, impact to loan forgiveness), because you can only consolidate once. Visit loanconsolidation.ed.gov for information on how you can consolidate your federal loans.

What's student loan forgiveness? It's when your remaining student loan debt is forgiven tax-free after ten years of public service (military, nurse, teacher). Check with your lender to see if you qualify for loan forgiveness. Visit finaid.org to learn more about this program.

Maria's Story

Maria entered the military. According to the Soldiers & Sailors Relief Act, all debts *prior* to being in the military can be reduced to a standard lower interest rate. So Maria wrote the various banks that she had accounts with and mailed the pertinent information to have her interest rates reduced. All creditors granted this act except one major bank. She continued to make her payments while she got the runaround to change that account's interest rate.

Maria could not get the bank to fix the issue and was always told that she did not include the correct information, even though she had included everything required. She recorded names, phone numbers, extensions, dates, and times of all phone calls. It didn't get rectified until nine months later when Maria got the help from a judge advocate general, who included all correspondence and the laws. The bank finally rectified and had to retroact it. By the time they made all of the adjustments, one of her accounts was nearly paid in full.

12. **Last but not least, remember to live below your means!** After all, it's the spending that got you into debt. Practicing self-control, discipline, and delayed gratification will help you spend less and pay off your debt more quickly. If you have problems using your credit cards, think of creative solutions to limit credit card use, such as cutting them up, using cash, or only carrying them on specific occasions (e.g., travel).

13. **Need Help?** If you need help, consider contacting the National Foundation for Credit Counseling (NFCC) for assistance at NFCC.org or (800) 388-2227. NFCC provides low-cost credit counseling services to help you with your debt.

Are You Thinking About Settling Your Debt?

It's best to follow through on your commitment to pay your creditor in full. However, if extenuating circumstances are preventing you from paying your account as agreed and you're thinking about settling your debt, then here's what you need to know *before settling*:

- **Do it yourself and avoid paying a debt settlement company to do it for you.**
- **Negotiate a repayment plan with your creditor before it goes to collections.** Creditors are usually easier to work with than debt collection agencies, so contact your creditor to discuss a repayment plan that works for you. Be upfront about any circumstances that are preventing you (e.g., unemployment) from paying as agreed.
- **Settling your account may negatively impact your credit report.** If your creditor agrees to accept less than the amount owed, it could be reported as settled and affect your credit score.
- **The IRS may treat any reduced debt as taxable income.** This means you could owe taxes on the amount of debt you were forgiven. Talk with a tax expert or visit irs.gov for the latest information on IRS rules and regulations.
- **Beware of creditors who ask for electronic access to your financial institution's account to settle.** Typically, creditors settle for an upfront lump sum cash amount only. For example, you may pay $400 (50–60% off) in cash on an outstanding balance of $900. In the event they agree to a payment plan and request electronic access to your account for withdrawals, *don't give it to them.* If you allow them to automatically withdraw money from your account, you no longer have control of when or how much you pay them unless you close the account.
- **Always get the settlement agreement (full terms) in writing before you settle your debt.** Any agreement that you make should be received in writing to ensure your creditor's commitment to the terms of your settlement.

Key Summary

- Drop the debt weight, so you can build wealth, improve your credit, and, most importantly, enjoy life without the financial stress.

- Your credit matters. Stay on top of your credit; get a free copy of your credit report and review it every year. Be sure to raise any reporting issues.

- Don't let money come between your relationships.

- Think positive and don't dwell on what you did wrong in the past.

- Be mindful of the financial decisions you make and carefully weigh the costs and benefits.

- Be committed to your debt-free action plan and find the courage to take action to achieve success.

Key #6

SAVE IN MORE WAYS THAN ONE

"If you would be wealthy, think of saving as well as getting."
–Benjamin Franklin

In today's economic times everyone's interested in saving money. How are you saving now? As you'll soon learn, you can definitely save in more ways than one.

My friends would tell you that I'm the person who knows how to save on just about anything, and I must admit they're absolutely right. I get really excited about saving money, and I love helping other people save too. In this key I'll reveal my money-saving strategies.

I've learned how to save money from people, good old-fashioned experience, and research. My friend Katina, for example, showed me the importance of saving for tomorrow. I met Katina while working at the bank. One day Katina asked me if I was going to participate in the savings programs at work. Basically, I responded, "Which one?" Working at a bank, there were so many to choose from. We had short-term options, such as stock purchase plans, and long-term options, such as retirement savings. Despite all of these options, my answer was an easy no, because I only saw them as another way to reduce my paycheck. Besides, I was young and a recent college grad, so why did I need to save now?

Katina's perspective was different from mine. Although we were close in age, she understood the value in saving to reach her short- and long-term goals. The way she viewed saving, the earlier you started, the better. In response to my decision, she simply smiled and tried to explain the benefits to me. I appreciated her interest in helping me, but I wasn't swayed. In my mind, my highest priority was to pay off my student loans. Period.

Over time, our friendship grew and we continued to talk about our finances. One day, Katina said, "Kembala, I'm so happy I finally saved enough money for a down payment on a new house."

This was great news, and I was excited for her. But I couldn't understand how she managed to save thousands of dollars. We worked the same job for about the same pay. However, I was single and living at home with my mom, while Katina was a single parent raising two young sons and renting an apartment. Yes, I was living below my means, paying bills and student loans on time and saving some money. But I needed to know what she was doing to save so much money, given her responsibilities. I asked her, "How'd you do it?"

Katina is one of the nicest people I've ever met, and she happily shared how she did it. She taught me how to save:
- Create a savings goal upfront and work toward it. Start by saving a small portion of every paycheck until you reach your goal.
- Contribute any additional income you may receive (e.g., bonuses) into savings.

- Shop smarter and use the money you save to reach your savings goal.
- Shop around for the best financial products. Katina was diligent about getting the best deals on her accounts. That's why she joined a credit union to refinance her auto loan for a lower interest rate and opened a new high-interest-bearing savings account.

Although she never mentioned this, I believe Katina's mindset and determination contributed to her success. She had a "can do" attitude. So she did it.

On the flip side, I've seen people who think they can't save, and it's true—they never manage to save anything. Could we be limiting ourselves with our minds? Absolutely, which is why having the right mindset is so important. I've helped clients who thought they couldn't save anything to change their mindsets and start doing what they never thought possible—saving. Amazingly, they went from having nothing to putting away thousands in savings within a year.

I'm very thankful for people like Katina who have used their experience to mentor me. In fact, Katina helped transform the way I thought about saving. As a result, I became an avid saver, and less than a year after our conversation, I had saved more than 20% of my salary.

In this chapter, we'll discuss how to save money in more ways than one. I'll show you how to:
- Build a personal savings emergency fund,
- Save for the future, and
- Shop smarter—save more, spend less.

Establish Your Personal Savings Emergency Fund

*"All days are not same. Save for a rainy day. When you
don't work, savings will work for you."*
–M.K. Soni

You've probably heard of "saving for a rainy day." It means you should save your money because you don't know what tomorrow may bring. There are many things that can happen to us that are beyond our control, but when you plan ahead financially it's easier to weather the storm. If you've ever been laid off or had an illness that kept you out of work, you probably know what I mean. Saving for a rainy day gives you financial security and lessens the load you have to carry when something unexpected happens.

Everyone needs to have a personal savings emergency fund to handle unforeseen expenses. If you don't have one, then this is a financial goal worth adding. You need to have at least seven months of your regular expenses in an emergency fund.

To save, you have to make it a priority. And "paying yourself first" helps ensure you do just that. Have you ever looked at your W-2 and asked yourself, where did all that money go? When you pay yourself first, you'll be able to have something to show for it. To pay yourself first, you set aside a portion of every paycheck for saving. You could also set this up automatically with your financial institution, so you won't even notice you're doing it.

The first step in setting up your personal emergency savings fund is to open your account. This account needs to be liquid, meaning it's accessible at any time without a penalty charge. Keep in mind this account is for emergencies only—for instance, if you lose your job, need a major home repair, or are forced to take time off work without pay. Whenever you use the funds in this account, it's important that you work toward building the account back up again after the event.

In my experience, I've found that online savings accounts typically offer better interest rates and lower fees. Remember to bank smart (see tips in "Key #3—Watch Where Your Money Goes . . . Literally!") and to choose a financial institution that works best for you. Check www.bankrate.com to compare interest rates and find out the minimum balance requirements to avoid monthly fees. Additional considerations for setting up your account include:

- Do you prefer banking locally? If so, does the bank you find online have local offices?
- Is interest compounded daily? Compounded interest means that you get interest on your total balance, which includes any interest that has been paid on your account. Interest may be compounded daily or monthly. It's best to have an account with daily interest compounding. This is how your money grows. Simple interest would only pay you interest on the money you contribute to the account and not on the accumulated interest.
- Are there any incentive offers for opening an account? When I opened a new money market account, I took advantage of a $100 incentive offer. Incentives are usually paid within a certain time after opening the account. However, the time passed, and I hadn't received my $100. So I stayed on top of it until I finally got my check. Make sure you receive any incentive they promise.
- Beware of monthly service charges. Your account shouldn't cost you more than you earn in interest. Watch your money closely to make sure this doesn't happen to you.

Be positive about being able to save, and you'll find creative ways to do so. For example, you could reduce your expenses and simplify your life. Make saving a habit. After all, saving helps you build financial security for tomorrow.

Save for the Future

"Failing to plan is planning to fail."
–Alan Lakein

When it comes to saving, are you a short-term or long-term thinker? As I mentioned earlier, I used to be very short-term focused. Then I learned the importance of being both. The personal savings emergency fund is intended to cover short-term needs. However, it's also important to save for your future.

 TIP

When it comes to saving for the future, it may be valuable for you to consult with a certified financial planner (CFP). A CFP will customize a plan based on your needs (e.g., insurance, investments) and where you are in life.

A big part of saving for the future is saving for retirement. Nice retirement packages and pension plans are a thing of the past for many of us, so saving for retirement is imperative. I've learned that we must take responsibility for our retirement. After all, no one else is going to do it for us. Are you saving for retirement?

Many people aren't saving for retirement, and some aren't even thinking about it. I've been there myself, because after college I thought it was just too far away. But the truth is, the earlier you start, the better, because your money will work for you and grow over a longer period of time.

While saving for retirement is a must, because you cannot take out a loan for your retirement, another area of financial concern is the cost of college. While college graduates can expect to earn more pay, the fact remains that tuition rates continue to climb. Therefore, it's important to plan and save for a college education. After all, at the time of this writing, the average college student graduates with about $24,000 in student loan debt. How's that for a graduation present? Personally, I can tell you student loan debt can be overwhelming.

Lastly, we'll discuss saving for large purchases. For example, you may want to purchase a home or car in a few years. Planning ahead for these types of purchases helps put you in a better financial position to make them.

Why Save for Retirement?

Planning for your retirement gives you more peace of mind and security. Employers have shifted away from pension plans, and we now have greater responsibility in planning and saving for a comfortable retirement. Therefore, we must take control of our financial futures.

Saving for your retirement is essential because people in the U.S. are living longer than they did in the past. According to the Centers for Disease Control, average life expectancy hit an all-time high in 2006 of 78.1 years.[17] Additionally, the cost of living keeps rising with healthcare, gas, and food costs going up.

---

17 Centers for Disease Control website, accessed April 17, 2011, http://www.cdc.gov/nchs/data/hus/hus08.pdf#026.

You may be asking, what about Social Security? Social Security, if you're unclear on what it is, is a U.S. federal social insurance program. Taxpayers fund Social Security through their payroll taxes (Federal Insurance Contributions Act, or FICA). Millions of Americans receive Social Security benefits, which fall under the categories of retirement, disability, and survivorship.

Many of the people who receive Social Security benefits are retired. That's why some people think Social Security will be enough to support them during retirement. However, Social Security was never intended to solely fund our retirements. It was meant to be the foundation on which our retirement savings, pensions, and/or investment income sits. According to the Social Security Administration, income from retirement benefits "replaces about 40 percent of an average wage earner's income after retiring."[18] This means that to retire comfortably you will need to save for retirement or have other sources of income (e.g., pension).

Social Security retirement benefits are calculated based on the amount of money earned over your working career and your age at the time that you start collecting benefits. You can start collecting as early as age 62. However, when you collect benefits early, they are reduced. If you delay your retirement and decide to collect benefits after your full retirement age, they are increased. For more details about your Social Security benefits, visit www.socialsecurity.com or call 800-772-1213.

Social Security most likely will not provide enough income to maintain your current lifestyle. Many people living on Social Secu-

---

18 Social Security website, accessed June 6, 2011,
    http://www.socialsecurity.gov/pubs/10024.html.

rity alone struggle to make ends meet. And some people are forced to make difficult choices between filling a prescription and putting food on the table, while others decide to return to work. Because of this, it's important to save for your retirement. In essence, saving for retirement is smart financial planning.

Retirement Savings Plans

Employer retirement savings plans (e.g., 401(k)) are probably the most popular savings option, because employers typically offer them in lieu of pension plans. The most common traditional retirement plans are:

- **401(k) retirement plan**—401(k) plans are set up by for-profit organizations.
- **403(b) retirement plan (also referred to as tax-sheltered annuity or TSA plans)**—403(b) plans are for employees of public schools and certain nonprofit organizations (hospitals, churches).
- **Thrift savings plan (TSP)**—TSPs are for federal employees (civil service) and members of the military.
- **457 plan (also known as "deferred compensation plans")**—457s are for employees of state and local government or certain nonprofit organizations.

IMPORTANT

> IRS rules and limits are subject to change, so visit irs.gov for the most recent information. Consult your tax attorney or certified public accountant (CPA) for further clarification and any tax questions.

Although the traditional retirement plans have different names, they typically work very similarly. Depending on your employer, you may be automatically enrolled or have to sign up to participate in your plan. Participating in these plans gives you an opportunity to contribute a portion of your compensation toward retirement.

The primary benefit of participating in traditional retirement plans is tax savings. When you participate, your contributions are usually automatically deducted from your paycheck as pre-tax dollars (before income taxes are deducted). And any profits you make on your investments are tax-deferred until withdrawal. In other words, you receive a tax break on your contributions the current year and you defer the taxes on your investment earnings until withdrawal. So your tax-free money grows in the account without incurring any taxes.

Because your contributions are tax-free, the IRS sets limits on the amount of money you can contribute every year. The 2011 limit is $16,500, but if you are 50 or older, you may be able to make catch-up contributions (additional money you can put toward retirement) of up to $22,000. However, your employer may set limits lower than these IRS contribution limits.

Some employers offer matching programs, in which your employer makes contributions toward your retirement when you do, up to a specific amount. For instance, your employer may contribute $0.50 for every dollar you put in, up to 7% of your salary. Say you earn a $55,000 salary. You decide to contribute 7%, which is $3,850, to your retirement plan, to take advantage of your employer's match program. Then your employer's matching contribution would be $1,925. This is like getting free money! So what are you waiting for? If your employer offers a match program, try to contribute up to that percentage if possible. If you're not able to contribute that amount yet, contribute what you can afford now, so you can start saving for your retirement. Then increase your contributions later when your income increases or financial situation improves.

Contact your employer's plan administrator or the benefits or human resources department to find out how your plan works. Keep in mind that retirement plans are made up of different investment options (e.g., mutual funds, stocks, bonds). Be sure to review your investment choices and any supporting information (e.g., reports) to help you make the best selections and manage your account.

 TIPS

- *For a glossary of investment terms, visit www.investopedia.com.*
- *If you receive a bonus, consider contributing some of it toward your retirement savings. This could reduce your taxes, and, more importantly, it helps you save for your financial future.*

Early Distributions

A withdrawal from your retirement account is called a distribution. Any withdrawal you make from your account prior to the age of 59½ (your age on the actual day of the withdrawal) is considered an early distribution. The withdrawal amount is treated as income for the current year. Because these accounts are intended to help you save for retirement, early distributions may be subject to an additional tax penalty of 10%. When you make early withdrawals from your retirement, you're limiting your financial security in the future, so carefully consider your options before taking an early distribution.

Hardship Distributions

You may be able to make a hardship withdrawal (referred to as a hardship distribution) from your retirement plan, provided your employer allows them and you meet the specified criteria. Plans vary, but examples may include paying medical expenses, paying educational expenses, or buying a new home. If you make a hardship withdrawal, the amount is treated as income for the current year. Also, you are subject to the IRS early distribution penalty of 10% if you are under the age of 59½.

Required Minimum Distributions

Generally, you must make required minimum distributions (RMD) from your account annually starting in the year you turn 70½, unless you meet IRS exception criteria that allow you to take these withdrawals later. If you don't take the entire required minimum distribution from your retirement account before the deadline, then you may have to pay a 50% tax on the amount not withdrawn. This is called the excess-accumulation penalty. For example, if the required minimum distribution is $15,000 on your account and you withdraw $10,000, the remaining $5,000 is subject to the 50% tax penalty. So you'd owe $2,500 to the IRS.

Retirement Plan Loans

Most retirement plans allow you to take out a loan against the funds in your plan provided you meet the plan's criteria. But beware of the consequences of taking out a retirement plan loan. After all, the purpose of contributing into your retirement plan is to have financial security in the future. And when you take out a loan against your account, you're limiting that security.

A friend asked me for my opinion on whether she should take out a loan against her 401(k) to pay off her high-interest credit card debt of $5,000. I recommended she consider other options, such as negotiating a lower interest rate or transferring her balance to another card. Here are five reasons for this:

1. Taking out a loan temporarily reduces the amount of money you have in your account, so you make less money in earnings.

2. This is treated as a loan. Therefore, you are expected to pay it back with interest. Although you are paying yourself back, you could incur lending costs such as loan initiation fees.

3. Your loan payment, which usually is automatically deducted from your paycheck, is made using after-tax dollars, whereas your contributions into a traditional retirement plan were originally tax-free.

4. Review the terms of the loan, because some employers may prevent you from participating in your retirement plan until the loan is paid back.

5. If you leave your employer (laid off, resigned, or fired), you may be required to pay the loan back in full immediately or within a short time (e.g., sixty days). If you're unable to pay, it will be considered an *early distribution.* This means the loan will be treated as income for the current year, so you'll have to pay income tax. Plus, you're subject to a 10% early distribution tax.

> *"Before you borrow from your 401(k) plan!*
> *Have you considered other loan sources? Borrowing from*
> *your plan may have a negative impact on the earnings of*
> *your account and reduce the money you will eventually have*
> *available for your retirement."*
> **–irs.gov 401(k) Resource Guide** [19]

Check with your retirement plan's administrator or the benefits or human resources department to find out how retirement plan loans and distributions work for your plan. Be sure to consider all of your options and the costs involved before you decide to borrow against your plan or make an early withdrawal.

---

19 IRS website, accessed June 6, 2011,
   http://www.irs.gov/retirement/participant/article/0,,id=151787,00.html.

Roth Retirement Plans

Your employer may offer you the option to contribute to a Roth 401(k), 403(b), or 457 plan. A Roth retirement plan offers you future tax savings if you expect to be in a higher tax bracket in the future. So, these retirement savings plans are great for young savers or anyone else who expects to be in a higher income bracket later. Unlike traditional retirement plans, Roth account contributions are made using after-tax dollars. This means that the contributions you make into a Roth retirement plan are not tax-deductible in the current year.

However, qualified distributions (withdrawals that meet IRS requirements) are tax-free. For example, if you are 59½ or older and have held your Roth account for five years at minimum, you could make a qualified distribution and it would be completely tax-free. On the other hand, if your withdrawal does not meet IRS requirements, it is called a nonqualified distribution. Nonqualified distributions are subject to income taxes on the investment earnings portion (because you used after-tax dollars to make your contributions) and may also be subject to an early distribution tax of 10%.

Roth retirement plans are similar to traditional retirement plans in that they have the same contribution limit amounts, require minimum distributions (RMD) starting at age 70½, and could allow you to take out loans and early distributions. If you do not make the RMD amount, you're subject to stiff tax penalties (see Retirement Plans—Required Minimum Distributions for details).

 TIP

Consult with a CPA or CFP to determine whether you should consider rolling over your Roth 401(k) to a Roth IRA (to be discussed later in this key), so you can avoid the required minimum distributions on your account.

It's important to note that you may make contributions into traditional and Roth retirement plans, but the total contribution must not exceed the IRS's maximum contribution limit, which is $16,500 or $22,000 (if you're 50 or older) in 2011. Roth plan participants may also benefit from employer match contributions, but employer deposits must be made into a pre-tax account (e.g., traditional 401(k)).

If your employer offers retirement plans, learn more about them. Ask questions, attend information seminars, and use any resources and tools available. Most importantly, take control of your financial future.

 TIP

Suppose you're considering rolling over your retirement plan into another retirement account. For example, if you leave your employer, you may decide to roll over your 401(k) into an IRA at a brokerage firm for lower fees. In this case, it's ideal to have your employer distribute funds directly into your designated eligible retirement account or IRA to avoid tax penalties. Consider consulting with a CPA, CFP or financial advisor you trust to help you determine the best option for you.

Individual Retirement Accounts

Individual retirement accounts (IRAs) are another option to save for retirement. These accounts, also known as "individual retirement arrangements" are definitely worth considering, especially if your employer doesn't offer a retirement plan or you're looking for more investment options to fund your retirement.

IRAs may be opened at many financial institutions and organizations, including banks and brokerage firms. They offer a variety of investment options. The two most popular IRAs are traditional IRAs and Roth IRAs.

IMPORTANT

IRS rules and limits are subject to change, so visit irs.gov for the most recent information. Consult your tax attorney, tax professional, or CPA for further clarification and any tax questions.

Traditional IRA

The major tax benefit of a traditional IRA is that your IRA earnings grow, tax-deferred. So, you don't pay any income taxes until you make a withdrawal from your account (called a distribution). Therefore, if you're in a lower tax bracket when you retire than you are today, you'll receive additional tax savings.

Your contributions into a traditional IRA may be tax deductible if you meet the IRS requirements. These requirements are based on your income, tax return filing status, and ability to contribute to an employer retirement plan. When you meet the IRS requirements, you can save for your retirement and receive a tax break because your contributions are tax-deductible in the current tax year. That's why many tax-cutting tips encourage you to open and fund your IRA account (if you qualify) before the tax filing due date.

You can contribute to a traditional IRA if you or your spouse made taxable compensation during the year and you were under the age of 70½ by the end of the year. The IRS sets contribution limits on these accounts. In 2011 IRA contribution limits are $5,000 per participant or $6,000 if you are 50 or older.

Similar to traditional retirement plans, traditional IRA accounts require you to receive minimum distributions (RMD) starting at the age of 70½, whether or not you need the money. If you do not make the RMD amount, you're subject to stiff tax penalties (see Retirement Plans—Required Minimum Distributions for details).

If you withdraw money from your IRA before the age of 59½ (called early distribution), the amount is treated as income and you may be subject to a 10% early withdrawal tax penalty.

Roth IRA

Contributions to Roth IRAs use after-tax dollars like a Roth retirement plan, so these contributions are not tax-deductible. However, your investment earnings grow tax-free. Plus, when you make qualified withdrawals (meet the IRS's Roth criteria for withdrawing funds) from your Roth IRA, they are tax-free income. So investing in a Roth IRA is a great option, if you think you may be in a higher tax bracket when you retire.

Another benefit of a Roth IRA is that there are no minimum required distributions. So you don't have to withdraw your money, and you can let your money grow tax-free.

Unlike Traditional IRAs, Roth IRAs do not have an age requirement to contribute, but you must meet certain income requirements. These IRS requirements are based on your taxable compensation, filing status, and modified adjusted gross income (AGI). In 2011, you cannot contribute into a Roth IRA if your modified AGI is $122,000 or more for single filing status and $179,000 or more for married.

The contribution limits for Roth IRAs in 2011 are $5,000 per participant or $6,000 if you are 50 or older.

If you make a nonqualified Roth IRA withdrawal, you may have to pay taxes on a portion of your withdrawal (based on earnings portion only, because you funded it with after-tax dollars) and the 10% early distribution tax.

Retirement Saver's Credit

If you make eligible contributions to your retirement plan or IRA and meet specific IRS requirements (e.g., age, income limits), you may be able to receive a retirement saver's credit on your federal taxes. In 2011, the credit is up $1,000 for filing single or up to $2,000 jointly.

Saving for College

In 2010, it was reported that for the first time, student loan debt exceeded credit card debt in the United States. That's not surprising, given that college education costs keep going up. I know how it feels to graduate from school with student loan debt. After I graduated from college, my student loan monthly payment was more than my car payment. That's a big deal when you're just starting out in the workforce.

So, what can you do to combat these high educational costs for your children or yourself? You can start saving for college now. There are many types of college saving plans:

- **Section 529 plan**—This is one of the most popular ways to save for college and other qualified education. 529 plans are managed by states and organizations, and anyone can set one up for a designated beneficiary. Contributions to a 529 are not tax-deductible. However, your investment earnings grow tax-deferred until withdrawn. And some states even offer tax incentives for in-state 529 participants. When you use your withdrawn money (distribution) for eligible education expenses, the money is not taxed as federal income, as it is with many retirement plans. There are two types of 529 plans (availability may vary by state):

a. Prepaid tuition savings plan—This gives you the opportunity to pay today's tuition rates for future tuition costs.

b. Savings plan—This is one of the most common options to save for a college education. This plan is used to fund tuition and other related college expenditures.

- **Coverdell education savings accounts**—These accounts are formally known as education IRAs. While contributions into this account are not tax deductible, earnings grow tax-deferred. If you make qualified withdrawals for education expenses (e.g., tuition, expenses) then the money is tax-free. Beneficiaries must be under 18 or have special needs, but distributions may be made until the beneficiary reaches 30. Contribution limits are set based on your income. In 2011, the income limits are based on a modified adjusted gross income of less than $110,000 (or $220,000 for a joint return). The maximum annual contribution per beneficiary is $2,000.

- **Uniform Gifts to Minors Act (UGMA) and Uniform Transfers To Minors Act (UTMA)**—These accounts are set up with cash and/or securities for minors. They are managed by a custodian but held in the minor's name. Therefore, any investment earnings subject to taxation are taxed at the child's income tax rate. Tax savings is the primary reason why people prefer the 529 and Coverdell college savings options, because investment earnings grow tax-free. Also, money held in a UGMA/UTMA account has a larger impact on financial aid eligibility since it is factored into financial aid calculations at a higher rate than other savings plans (e.g., 529).

- **Credit card rebate programs**—Another way to save for college is to register your credit cards with an organization (e.g., Upromise, BabyMint) that contributes money toward college savings when you shop at certain retailers or purchase specific products. To learn more about these free programs, visit finaid.org.

For more detailed information on how you can save for college, visit the websites below:

- www.fastweb.com
- www.finaid.org
- www.savingforcollege.com
- www.scholarshipexperts.com

Financial aid, scholarships, and grants can definitely help you minimize your college education costs. If you're willing to spend the time researching scholarships, it could save you money. However, beware of college scholarship scams. You should not have to pay money to receive a scholarship. Always remember, if the offer sounds too good to be true, it probably is. Visit www.ftc.gov for tips on how you can avoid scholarship scams.

Large Purchases

My husband, Sam, thought it would be a good idea to include saving for large purchases in this section. After all, these purchases are the main reasons some of us are in debt today. I consider a large purchase to be anything that costs more than $500. How do you pay for these types of purchases? Do you "buy now, pay later"? If so, I urge you to adopt a new way of buying, in which you "think about it, save for it, and then buy it."

This approach makes it easier for you to:

- Use the extra time to think through your purchase. Is it really something you need?
- Take time to shop around and compare.
- Stay out of debt. It's nice to purchase something without dreading the bill in the mail.
- Appreciate your purchase more because you delayed gratification.
- Save money. Paying with cash may give you additional savings. For example, when I bought my furniture, I received 15% off for paying with cash.

Saving for large purchases is the way to go. The benefits are tremendous, and practicing this money principle will put you on a quicker path to *Get Your Money Right!*

Shop Smarter

> *"If you can, you will quickly find that the greatest rate of return you will earn is on your own personal spending. Being a smart shopper is the first step to getting rich."*
> **–Mark Cuban**

When my husband and I got married we quickly noticed the major difference in the way each of us shopped. Sam knew specifically what he needed to buy before he went to the store. At the store, he focused on the specific item(s) and easily avoided impulse purchases. He would get what he needed and proceed to the checkout. Overall, Sam's way of shopping was much quicker and cost effective than mine. However, I noticed that he rarely took the time to look through sale or clearance items because he had a laser-sharp focus on his item(s) only.

When it came to my way of shopping, I usually had an idea of what I wanted to buy before I headed out to the store. I took a more leisurely approach inside the store, checking out the new styles and fashions. However, I always sought to make my purchases from the discount or clearance racks because I never wanted to pay retail. As I perused the racks, I chose items that met one of two criteria: satisfied my original shopping intent or appeared to be a good deal. Sam absolutely hated the way I shopped because it was very time consuming and less orderly. Sometimes I would say I'm going to one store and end up in three to five other stores on the same trip. It was the unpredictability and the time I spent in stores that Sam disliked most. Sound familiar?

Since then, we've found a happy medium. Some of the changes we've made:

- Create a shopping list and adhere to that list despite any luring sales signs.
- When shopping for clothing or shoes, check out the sale and clearance items, especially at the end of a season, to get rock-bottom prices.
- Be more efficient shoppers by focusing on our needs and initial shopping destinations (no distractions), because there is definitely a correlation between the time spent in a store and how much money you spend. Think about that when you are in and out quickly. You usually purchase less and only what you need, right?

Becoming a smart shopper is an important part of saving, because the money you save will help you build wealth.

Clothing and Shoes

Shopping smart does not just mean you make your purchasing decisions based on price. A smart shopper looks at value. Shopping for value may cost you a little more today, but it saves you more money in the long run because you don't have to buy the same thing over and over again. It makes more sense to buy higher quality items at a discount price. And higher quality does not equate to brands; it is more determined by the materials, look, and detail of the product. Here are some tips on how to save on clothing and shoes:

- **Buy used.** A lot of money can be saved if you don't mind shopping at a consignment shop, garage sale, or other second-hand place.
- **Use coupons and free money offers.** Sales combined with money-saving coupons can make store prices more affordable. Sometimes I get free money offers (e.g., $10 off gift cards) during holidays, and I often use these to purchase things I need at a discounted price.
- **Look for sale and clearance items.** Some of the best deals I have ever received came from department stores with drastically reduced clearance items, especially during end-of-season markdowns. That's the best time to pick up higher quality items at deeply discounted prices.
- **Shop at outlets and discount stores.** In my experience, some outlets are truly worthy of the name and others never seem to live up to it. Before shopping at these centers it's a good idea to become familiar with normal store prices, so that you can spot the real deals. Also, look out for coupon books and VIP deals that provide additional savings. If you plan ahead, you can usually find these types of offers on outlet malls' websites free. Look for additional savings at information booths too. Discount stores such as Marshall's, Nordstrom Rack, Off 5th, Ross, SYMS, and Loehmann's also can offer you great bargains.

- **Shop online.** You can find a lot of great deals on the Web.
- **Join loyalty programs.** Many stores offer customer loyalty programs and coupon offers if you sign up for their mailing lists.
- **Repair shoes.** Sometimes it's hard to find good shoes. When you have a nice pair that is worn, consider getting them repaired instead of buying new ones.

Groceries

- **Plan ahead.** Create a grocery list and stick with it in the store. This helps you identify the items you need and saves time. Planning ahead reduces the chances of eating out or having to make short grocery runs later in the week.
- **Avoid impulse purchases.** Research shows the longer you shop, the more money you spend. That's why planning ahead and using a shopping list helps you get in and out of the store more quickly. I know those displays and the big sale prices can be a real draw, but do you really need that?
- **Use coupons and sign up for grocery card discount programs.** If I expressed the value of a coupon as a math equation, it would be COUPON = FREE MONEY. Some of my favorite places to get coupons are:
  - **Newspaper.** Sunday newspapers are usually filled with coupons. You may want to consider purchasing a newspaper subscription. Money saved using coupons regularly should more than pay for the subscription. It's best to get a subscription for the Sunday newspaper, but it's often cheaper to get multiple days.
  - **From the store.** Some stores offer savings with their own coupons. You may find them on the store's website, in ads, in the newspaper, during checkout, or through the store's preferred card program. These coupons have the store's name printed on them and do not say "manufacturer's cou-

pon." If you sign up for the store's discount program you may receive coupon offers and special member pricing.

- **Inside the store**—The best place to look for coupons in the store are in the weekly store ads. You may also find them in the coupon dispensers placed in aisles, on tear pads near the items, or directly on the item you are purchasing. It amazes me to see people who purchase an item with a $1- or $2-off coupon stuck on it that they never even peel off.
- **Internet**—The Internet is filled with coupons. Many stores, manufacturers, and coupon-specific websites offer printable coupons. A few sites to try are: CouponMom.com, Smart-Source.com, RedPlum.com, and Coupons.com.

- **Maximize your coupons**. Maximizing your coupons could cut your grocery bill in half:
  - **Combine store and manufacturer coupons**—For example, if you have a manufacturer's coupon for $1.00 off peanuts and a store coupon for $1.00 off that same brand of peanuts, most stores allow you to use both and receive $2.00 off your peanuts.
  - **Use coupons on clearance items**—Save more by using coupons on clearance and sale items.
  - **Take advantage of double- or triple-coupon offers**—You can really put coupons to work during double- or triple-coupon store events. When the retailer doubles or triples the value of a coupon it could easily turn into free purchases.

One day when I went to a Kmart double-coupon event, a sales clerk said, "You did well, but I had a customer earlier today who was unbelievable in maximizing her double-coupon savings!" He told me this customer had two shopping carts full of items. There were so many items and coupons that it took him over an hour to ring her up. The real amazement came when he told me her $300-plus bill shrank down to less than $5 after he scanned all of her coupons. Can you imagine that? I still find it hard to believe, but he told me it was true and that the woman learned all about couponing from Jill Cataldo, the Super-Coupon Queen.

 TIP

Read the fine print. Check for any restrictions—expiration date, limit, product descriptions, minimum purchase requirement, and coupon exclusions.

- **Shop on sale days.** Some stores offer special sales on certain days—Sunday through Wednesday or during holidays. Bargain sales may last a few days only, such as Sunday and Monday. Check weekly ads to find out about special sales offers. This is another reason newspapers are handy.

  Grocery store sales are important because they help you maximize your savings. Say a box of cereal is on sale for $2.00 and you use a $1.50 coupon. Then you pay $0.50. If you bought the same cereal for $3.69 and used your same coupon it would have cost you $2.19.

- **Save your paper and plastic money for future purchases.** Some rewards programs give you money back in receipt form or gift cards toward your next purchase. Be sure to save these and use them before they expire on future purchases. This is free money, so use it!

- **Grow your own garden and save green.** Growing your own garden can help reduce your food costs.

- **Check to make sure the price you pay is right.** As discussed in "Key #3 Watch Where Your Money Goes...Literally," if you check your receipt you can avoid being overcharged. Some stores give you the item free when it rings up incorrectly.
- **Bigger does not always mean the better value.** Sometimes we think the largest size has the best price. But this is not always true. Some stores show you the price-per-unit calculation, which is very helpful in determining the most value for your money. If your store does not provide this calculation, bring your calculator to determine the cheapest option. You simply divide the price (e.g., $6.99) by the unit size (e.g., 100 oz.), and the lowest price per unit is the best value.

 TIP

Be sure to take into account any sale price or coupons you may have when calculating it yourself.

- **Check the expiration date of items before purchasing them.**
- **Buy in bulk.** Purchasing items (e.g., toilet paper, snack bars) in bulk could save you money. It depends on the type of product, your level of use, and the expiration date. Be sure to do the math to make sure it's a better deal.

Medical and Insurance Costs

- **Understand how your benefits work.** The ability to participate in employer life insurance, medical, and dental coverage at discounted group rates is a great benefit. That's why they are called "benefits." Review your employer's benefits package and select the best options for you. Understand how your benefits work so that you can make sure you receive the correct coverage. For example, I learned from a coworker that our medical plan covered vision services. I had been paying a discounted rate for my eye exams, glasses, and contacts when I could have been claiming them for reimbursement with my insurance.

- **What's the better deal, term life insurance or whole life insurance?** Life insurance is essential, because it provides your family with financial security when you die. A term life insurance policy provides you with coverage at a fixed rate for a fixed period of time. For example, a $500,000 twenty-year term policy may cost $295 annually. On the other hand, a whole life insurance policy combines life insurance coverage with savings and carries a cash value, so premiums tend to be much higher. I think term life insurance is better because it offers you the coverage you need for less (lower premiums), so you can take your cost savings difference and invest it yourself. Besides, you have more investment options available outside of a whole life policy anyway.

- **Shop around for lower insurance rates.** Even if you already have auto, life, home, or any other type of insurance policy, you may find a better deal when you shop around for comparable insurance (be sure to get the best coverage for you) with other reputable providers. The Internet makes it easy to do. Insurance rates fluctuate, and providers charge different rates for the same level of coverage. That's why companies encourage you to get rate quotes, because a new policy could save you quite a bit of money and may even provide more coverage. After all, those ads that tell you customers who switched to Company X saved $500 had to get their data from somewhere. A little bit of time could save you quite a bit of money.

- **Increase your deductibles and get discounts.** Increasing your deductible normally reduces your premium. However, before you do this, make sure the new deductible is something you are comfortable paying in the event something happens. Also, are you getting all your discounts? There are so many discounts you could qualify for, such as good driving record, good student, alarm system, multiple policies, group, and more. Give your insurance provider a call to make sure you are maximizing your discounts.

 TIP

Another savings opportunity is to pay your insurance premiums annually or semi-annually if you can afford it. This helps you avoid the monthly payment charge.

- **Exercise.** Be sure to consult your doctor before you start any exercise program. Exercising helps you stay fit and feel better. Being in good health saves you money in medical and insurance costs.
- **Explore long-term disability insurance.** Consider long-term disability insurance if it's available at a reasonable cost. It can really help (check coverage) if you have a health condition that forces you to take a large amount of time off work.
- **Negotiate medical bills.** If you are uninsured, try negotiating the cost of a medical procedure in advance.
- **Save on your prescriptions:**
  - Ask the doctor for samples.
  - Purchase generic drugs, which can offer you savings over brand names. Check with your doctor to make sure it's OK first.
  - Order drugs through the mail. Before I fill a prescription I normally ask how much the drug will cost. One day I was alarmed to find out a prescription drug cost more than $100. I called my benefits department and found out it could be drastically reduced if I ordered it through the mail, and I did just that. You can also look for opportunities to buy a ninety-day supply over a thirty-day supply for additional cost savings.

- Take advantage of $4 prescription drugs and new/transfer prescription gift card offers. Some retailers offer hundreds of drugs for $4. Check your local pharmacies for any special pricing. If you're starting a new prescription somewhere, see if they are offering a free gift card. Some pharmacies offer you a $25 gift card for a new or transferred prescription.

Gas

- **Limit driving.** Use public transit, carpool, bike, or walk if possible. This will lessen the wear and tear on your car and reduce gas costs.
- **Maintain your vehicle.** Check your car maintenance guide to properly maintain your car. This includes getting regular oil changes, checking your tire pressure, changing your air filter and sparkplugs (as needed), and getting regular tune-ups.
- **Drive the speed limit.** Believe it or not, it's been proved that driving the speed limit improves your gas mileage.
- **Reduce idle time and use cruise control on the highway.** If you spend more than a minute in idle you are burning gas at 0 mpg. Turn off your engine to save gas. Use cruise control when you can to maintain a constant speed for more fuel efficiency.
- **Get rid of that junk in your trunk.** A heavier car will reduce your fuel efficiency.
- **Bundle errands to reduce the number of trips.** Grouping car trips together will save you money at the pump.
- **Don't buy premium gas, unless your car requires it.** The cost difference between regular unleaded and premium can be more than $0.20 a gallon, which can quickly add up. Check your owner's manual—if it recommends regular gas, buy it and save your money. According to ftc.gov, "Using a higher octane gas than recommended offers no benefit—and costs you at the

pump. Unless your engine is knocking, buying higher octane gas is a waste of money."[20]

General Purchases

- **Join a wholesale club.** This can save you a lot of money in a variety of categories, such as travel, gas, grocery, home, and landscaping products. Some clubs even offer you coupons for additional savings.

 TIP

Check with your employer or other affiliations (e.g., credit card) for discounted membership opportunities.

- **Pass on by those impulse purchases.** My friend Monica is very conservative, but she confessed to me that she really struggles with impulse buying. When the big price in red catches her attention, she feels like the signs are saying, "Buy me, buy me." She's right—it can be difficult to pass up what appears to be a bargain. However, making impulse purchases results in higher bills at the checkout lane. Do you understand Monica's challenge?

I told her to learn to **pass it on by**! Old habits may seem to be hard to break, but changing the way you do things often leads to more success. After all, if you didn't need it before you went to the store, then you probably don't need it as you're leaving. Resist the urge to buy it just because it's a deal. Change your way of thinking and your actions will soon follow—as you pass it on by! Simply smile to yourself and say, "I'm not falling for it this

---

20 Federal Trade Commission website, accessed June 6, 2011, http://www.ftc.gov/bcp/edu/pubs/consumer/autos/aut12.shtm.

time." You'll see that this strategy will help you keep more money in your pocket.

- **Just say no! Politely.** Do you have a problem saying no to the salespeople in your life? Whether it is a telemarketer on the phone or the nice person who just rang your doorbell. If it's not something you need, you can be polite and say "No thank you." When the rebuttals come, firmly respond, "Thanks for the offer, but I really don't need it."

 TIP

To sign up for the Do Not Call List online, go to www.donotcall.gov. To sign up by phone, call 888-382-1222.

- **Use card benefit programs to make big purchases.** Using your rewards to get cash back or other benefits can be another way to save on your purchase.
- **Use coupons on online purchases.** Whenever I make a purchase online, I look for an online coupon first. Doing this helps me save money about 85% of the time. I simply type the store name plus "online coupon" or the store name plus "promotion code" in a search engine and look through the results.
- **Take care of what you have now.** You have the opportunity to save more over the long run when you take care of the things you have now. For example, if you take care of your car by having regular maintenance, then you are more likely to reduce your costs and drive it longer.
- **Get organized.** You save money when you're organized. Have you ever bought something to find out you already had it at home? Plus, organization can pay off when it comes to tax deductions, too.

- **Don't buy lottery tickets.** Playing the lottery is not the way to build wealth. The odds of winning are just too slim. Remember what Warren Buffet says about investing, especially rule #1 ("Key #3—Watch where your money goes . . . literally!").
- **Carefully examine rent-to-own schemes.** You know the rent-to-own offers in which you rent a laptop for the low weekly price of $24.99 with the chance to own? These deals may seem attractive at a glance, but look closer at the numbers and terms. You may be surprised to see you could be paying double or triple the normal cost of such items. After all, these places are in business for a reason—to make money. Besides, many of them do not check your credit, which may sound good on the surface, but it means everyone pays more to account for the risk. If you need it now, consider buying it used. Most importantly, look at the math to see if it's a rental rip-off.

Mortgage

- **Shop around and compare different lenders.** Visit Bankrate. com to compare competitive interest rates in your area. Check with lenders and review their good-faith estimates to evaluate the mortgage terms (i.e., interest rate, expected closing costs).
- **Consider refinancing to get a fixed-rate mortgage, take advantage of lower interest rates, or reduce your loan term.** Refinancing can lower your monthly payment and reduce the interest you pay over the life of the loan. Some considerations before refinancing:
  - Remember fixed rates are easier to project the long-term costs of. And keep in mind you may intend to stay somewhere for two years and end up being there for twenty years.
  - Understand the costs and benefits before refinancing. Will your interest rate be lower? How much will your monthly savings be? How much are the closing costs? Will you have

a prepayment penalty? As mentioned in "Key #5—Drop the Debt Weight," refinance calculators are helpful.

Save on Services

Many services offer coupon savings in phone books, flyers, magazines, promotional mail inserts, and online. Keep in mind that when you are using service providers (e.g., a house painter), you may be able to negotiate a lower price. Following are some other tips to help you save on services.

Travel

- **Plan early to get better savings on travel itinerary.** The earlier you book, the more opportunity you have to save when traveling in the United States. Preferably, book at least two weeks in advance.
- **Shop around.** Compare the prices on travel websites, but remember some airlines are not available on these sites. Besides, the lowest price may be found on the official airline website, so compare these prices as well. Here's a list of popular travel sites:
  - expedia.com
  - hotwire.com
  - orbitz.com
  - priceline.com
  - tripadvisor.com

 TIP

Beware of extra fees (e.g., baggage charges) and travel cancellation policies when booking.

- **Discounts, coupons, and promotion codes.** Applying discounts, coupons, or promotions can translate into big savings on travel. For example, my warehouse club membership comes with travel discounts, and I got 25% off normal rental car rates plus a day free.

Discounts may be offered on rental cars, hotels, airfare, trains, and various other travel-related expenses. A few examples of those who may qualify for discounts are special organization members, college students, senior citizens, employees of certain companies, or members of the military. Coupons and promotion codes may be available on the Web (company sites, social media sites, motor club sites) or through warehouse club travel services, credit card promotions, or your car insurance provider.

 TIP

Employer discounts can be very valuable during peak travel. For instance, one Christmas I used my company's contracted rate to avoid outrageous rental car rates.

- **Buy airline tickets earlier in the week.** When it comes to buying your airline ticket, it's best to buy it earlier in the week instead of on the weekend. Travel experts say tickets tend to be cheaper on Tuesdays and Wednesdays. If you're debating a purchase, you may want to put it on hold because prices can fluctuate even throughout the day.
- **Join frequent traveler programs.** Frequent traveler programs can help you save on fees (e.g., baggage), get travel perks (e.g., special offers, upgrades, priority boarding), and receive free travel benefits (hotel stays, tickets).
- **Travel during off-peak times.** Traveling on off-peak days (Tuesdays, Wednesdays, and Saturdays) can save you money on your airline tickets. Early-morning or late-night flights may also be cheaper. Switching your travel date by a day or two could amount to hundreds of dollars in savings.

- **Compare package deals.** Bundling your travel into a package (airline, hotel, and rental car) could offer tremendous savings.
- **Purchase a travel pass.** If you are planning on visiting a city and touring some of the major attractions, travel passes can really save you money. My husband and I purchased a city pass in San Francisco, and it included all of the attractions we wanted to visit and public transportation, amounting to about 50% in total savings.

Entertainment
- **Look for opening night show discounts and other savings opportunities**. Some events, such as circuses, ice shows, and plays, offer deeply discounted tickets (flat-rate seats) on opening night. Plan ahead and purchase your tickets early and save! You can also look for group ticket discounts.
- **Eat at home, but if you have to eat out, use coupons.** Coupons come in handy when dining out. You can find coupons on sites like Restaurant.com and in newspapers and entertainment coupon books. Also, if you have a family, kids-eat-free offers are great.
- **Enjoy free entertainment.** The Internet and local news are great ways to find out about free events in your area. Take advantage of free days at museums, festivals, and other public venues. Also, go to libraries and parks. Libraries and park districts offer free programs and activities for the entire family.
- **Save on your movies.** Check out movie deals on off-peak hours, such as first showings or before-noon specials. Also consider checking out movies from the library or using low-cost rental options like Redbox and Netflix. You could also borrow them from your friends.
- **Buy entertainment ticket deals at your wholesale club.** I've seen deeply discounted restaurant gift cards, movie tickets, and other entertainment packages at my club.

Utilities

- **Purchase a programmable thermostat.** This helps you save energy and control the temperature based on your schedule.
- **Purchase energy-efficient products.** These types of products are clearly marked with the ENERGY STAR label. When it comes to light bulbs, these may cost more initially, but they last longer and use less energy. Energy-efficient appliances and computers also save you money on your utilities bills. You may also want to consider changing your toilets or showerheads to reduce your water use.

 TIP

Depending on the type of purchase and purchase date you may be able to receive tax savings benefits. Check with your state for any energy efficiency tax savings programs. Visit irs.gov or talk with your tax advisor to find out more on energy tax savings.

- **Other ways to save money on your energy bills.** Caulk or upgrade your windows to help insulate your home and save you money on electric and gas bills. Turn off lights when you leave the room. Turn off the television and computers. Change your air filters, insulate the attic, insulate your water heater, wash clothes in cold water, and fix leaks.

Flexible Spending Accounts

A flexible spending account (FSA) is a benefit option provided through your employer. Money contributions into an FSA receive a tax benefit, because it uses pre-tax dollars and withdrawals from the account are not taxed. Therefore, the IRS clearly outlines the specific guidelines for contribution limits and qualified expenses under the program. Your contributions to an FSA are automatically deducted from your paycheck. There are two types of flexible spending accounts: health care expenses (e.g., eye exams) and dependent care expenses (e.g., childcare).

Be sure to familiarize yourself with the qualified expenses and the program details before enrolling. It is very important to estimate reasonable amounts to set aside for such expenses, because these accounts operate on a "use it or lose it" rule. In other words, if you do not use all of the money in your account on qualified expenses by the specified date, then you lose it. Your employer may have expense estimate calculators to assist you in estimating such expenditures. Check with your human resources or benefits department for more information on the program.

As with any reimbursement programs, be sure to keep your receipts and follow the reimbursement submission process. This will make it easier for you to be reimbursed. Remember the goal is to save money, not lose it.

 TIPS
- *Revisit your FSA if you have a qualifying life event (e.g., marriage, birth of a baby). For example, if you have a baby, you will have daycare expenses in the current year.*
- *Visit www.irs.gov for the latest information on FSA tax benefits.*

Phone
- **Shop around to compare the competition.**
- **Take advantage of any discounts you qualify for.** This could include employee discounts at your company.
- **Bundle for greater savings.** Consider combining Internet, phone, and cable for deeper discounts.
- **Check your cell phone use and adjust your plan if you need to.** Check your cell phone use to determine whether you have

the best plan for your calling patterns. If you have a sudden spike in use, call your provider quickly. They may be able to upgrade your plan or sell you minutes to cover you for the current month, so you don't get cell phone bill shock.

Dry Cleaning

- **Ask if they will honor competitor coupons.** You may be surprised by their answer.
- **Evaluate the quality.** Cheaper does not mean better. A low-quality cleaner could cost you more in the end.
- **Shop for easy-care clothing that does not require dry cleaning.**
- **Discover Woolite or do it yourself dry cleaning products.** This may save you money on some of your dry cleaning costs.

Home

- **Learn to do it yourself.** If you're handy around the house, it could save you money. And you may even use your skills to generate additional income. Get the information and supplies you need from your local home improvement stores such as Ace Hardware, The Home Depot, or Lowe's. Another useful source for fix-it information is the Internet. Simply type what you're looking for into your favorite search engine, and you'll find all types of helpful information such as discussion forums, product user guides, step-by-step instructions, and demonstration videos.
- **Keep up with routine maintenance.** Maintaining your home can save you money in repairs and high energy bills.
- **Property tax assessments.** If you're a homeowner, you could be saving money on your property taxes. Review your property appraisal and tax assessment information. Next, compare (e.g., sales, size) it with other houses in your area. This information may be available on your property tax and appraisal websites.

If you find your taxes to be high, then appeal them using the property tax appeal process. Be sure to use the research information you have collected. I've always filed my own appeals, and the process is easy to do in my area. If you don't have the time, you may want to use a tax attorney or consultant.

Shipping

When it comes to shipping, our first inclination may be to go with a specific carrier only, but you'd be surprised to see the savings you may be missing out on by not shopping around. And it's easy to do; just compare prices online using your shipping information (e.g., zip code, weight, size). Some carriers to consider:

- www.fedex.com
- www.ups.com
- www.usps.com

Whether it's a birthday gift or documents that need to be sent overnight, the shipping costs could be significantly different across carriers. This past Christmas, my daughters received Pillow Pets and the shipping cost nearly as much as the gift. During peak seasonal shopping periods like Christmas, it's best to take advantage of free shipping or low online shipping offers.

Key Summary

- If you think you can save, you will.

- Build your personal savings emergency fund with seven months of expenses.

- Save for your retirement—take control of your financial future!

- College savings plans could offer you tax savings.

- Shop smart and save on practically anything. The more you save, the more you'll have to pay off debt and invest in the future.

Key #7

BE GRATEFUL AND GIVE FREELY

"Blessed are those who can give without remembering and receive without forgetting."
– Unknown

The final key to unlocking a better financial future is—be grateful and give freely. I believe there's power behind the acts of gratitude and giving. That's why I call it the power of Gs. Are you living and practicing the power of Gs today? If not, I hope these words inspire you to put the power of Gs into action in your life.

When we show gratitude for what we have, we tend to live happier and fuller lives. While generosity has an amazing two-way effect on the giver and receiver. Have you ever noticed that?

Speaking of giving, do you know what it means to give freely? A person who gives freely does so from the heart without expecting anything in return.

In this chapter we'll take a closer look at the power of Gs—gratitude and giving. After all, the power of Gs opens the door for more abundance in your life.

Be Grateful for What You Have

"A grateful mind is a great mind
that eventually attracts to it great things."
–Plato

Do you consider yourself a grateful person? Are you someone who focuses on what's missing? Do you find yourself comparing what you have and where you are in life to others? Depending on your answers to those questions, you fall into one of the following categories: grateful, kind of grateful, or ungrateful.

If you're a grateful person, that's wonderful, because your attitude brings good things into your life. If you landed in the kind of grateful or ungrateful categories, the good news is that having this awareness will help you drive change in your life. Remember that everything stems from your mindset, so develop an attitude of gratitude to change your direction. The easiest way to change is to shift your focus away from what you may be lacking to what you already have to be thankful for now. As you do this, you'll soon find you have more to be grateful for than you may have thought.

I've learned the importance of being grateful throughout my life experience. Perhaps my mother instilled it in me by the way she lived her life. As a child I learned to appreciate even the smallest things. For example, when I was in middle school I remember the time I took my little sister out to dinner. I was so excited that my mother let us go out to dinner on our own. I planned ahead to make sure we had enough money to pay for our food and the waitress's tip. After we ate and paid for our dinner, I noticed a little problem. I had spent all of the money on our dinner and did not have a quarter to call my mom to pick us up. I could not believe I forgot the quarter. I started to think about my dilemma and how I might not have been in the situation had I left the waitress one less quarter. Then I decided to look in the pay phone's coin return for any leftover change. Surprisingly, I found the quarter I needed. I was so thankful for that shiny quarter that day—you would have thought I had won a prize. If you're thankful for the small things, then they will turn into bigger things later.

No one is perfect, and there have surely been occasions when I have appeared ungrateful. In those moments, I'm most thankful for my husband, Sam, who lets me know so I can correct the situation.

When it comes to gratitude, it's important to appreciate what you have now, which can be challenging if you let what you *don't* have get in the way. When you look beyond the unfavorable circumstances you might have, I'm sure you'll find many people and things you have to be thankful for, such as your family, friends, and health. Besides, thinking about what you have to be thankful for always seems to make the situation better.

Yes, we are all human, and there may be times when we take what we have for granted. For instance, a friend told me the other day how upset he was to have to go into work for a meeting on his day off. This conversation took place when the unemployment rate was hovering around 9%. Needless to say, I was not sympathetic.

I asked him, "Do you know how fortunate you are to be able to go to work? There are many people who wish they had a job to go to right now."

This changed his perspective, and suddenly that meeting didn't seem so bad. He agreed and said he was glad he had a job.

If we take a step back and look at our situations a little differently, we may find that we have a lot more than we think to be thankful for. Many examples of this come to mind. You have the wife who complains about her husband and the single woman who wishes she had someone to share her life with. Perhaps it could be the parent who is unhappy with his child struggling in school and the couple across the street praying just to conceive a child. The list goes on and on. Sometimes we don't value what we have until it's gone or something drastic happens to help us realize its significance. Don't let that be you. Learn to be grateful for the people and things you have in your life.

> *"Not that I speak in respect of want: for I have learned, in whatsoever state I am, therewith to be content."*
> **–Philippians 4:11 (King James Version)**

Attitude of Gratitude Story

Auntie Ginny went on a seven-day Caribbean cruise. Her trip was filled with walks in paradise, great food, a variety of activities, and spectacular entertainment. While she toured beautiful islands and met wonderful people, she thought about her nieces. When she stepped out during a port call in Jamaica, she thought of them even more as she saw beautiful vibrant sundresses hanging in the open marketplace. She imagined how pretty the girls would look in the dresses and their happy faces when they would receive them. That picture brightened her day and she bought two pretty hot pink sundresses. She was certain her nieces would like them as much as she did. As her nice relaxing trip came close to an end, she got so excited about surprising her nieces with the lovely sundresses and could hardly wait to see them.

The day after her return, she visited her nieces to show them pictures from the trip. Her sister and niece Yasmine were the only ones home at the time, so Auntie Ginny gave Yasmine her gift. As soon as she gave it to Yasmine, Yasmine hugged her and said "Thanks for thinking of me on your trip, Auntie Ginny. We really missed you." She opened the gift and absolutely loved the dress. She shook it up and down, asking her mother if she could go and try it on. After putting on the dress, Yasmine began modeling it with the biggest smile and said it was a perfect fit. Her happiness was all over her face, and she thanked her auntie again, showering her with hugs and kisses.

Later that day, Yasmine's sister, Rachel, came home. Auntie Ginny could not wait to give her the gift. Rachel quickly opened it to see what was inside. After she pulled through all of the tissue paper, she shouted, "Pink! I am so tired of pink. Why didn't you get me purple or some other color?" In disappointment, she abruptly handed the dress back to her auntie and walked away hastily. Auntie Ginny was shocked and saddened by her response. She gazed down at the dress in disbelief about what had just occurred. Yasmine peered around the corner and could sense her disappointment. In an effort to comfort her, Yasmine gave her a nice big hug as she whispered, "Thanks for giving us both such nice dresses. I am sure Rachel will wear hers too."

Please take a moment and reflect on the short story above. Do you see the difference an attitude of gratitude can make?

This story makes it easy to distinguish grateful and ungrateful actions. Would you agree that people are more likely to do more for you when you show appreciation and gratitude for their acts of kindness? When gratitude is missing they may not feel as compelled to do something in the future. After all, most people have an inherent desire to feel appreciated. When you appreciate what you have, you value it and take care of it, and as a result, it tends to last longer. Whether it's things or relationships, an attitude of gratitude can make a big difference.

What causes us to be ungrateful? While there are many reasons, comparing yourself to others is probably one of the biggest. When you constantly compare what you have or where you are in life with other people, it creates dissatisfaction and unhappiness inside. Then you start focusing on what you don't have, because you're putting all the negative energy on what you lack and losing sight of what you already have. As Ken Keyes, Jr. once said, "To be upset over what you don't have is to waste what you do have."

If this is you, I strongly urge you to stop comparing and be grateful and appreciative for the things you do have. That may be a loved one, a car to drive, or legs to walk with. No matter how small or big, showing appreciation for what you have will bring you more.

> *"Be thankful for what you have; you'll end up having more.*
> *If you concentrate on what you don't have,*
> *you will never, ever have enough."*
> **–Oprah Winfrey**

Give Freely

> *"One man gives freely, yet gains even more; another withholds*
> *unduly, but comes to poverty. A generous man will prosper;*
> *he who refreshes others will himself be refreshed."*
> **–Proverbs 11:24-25 (NIV)**

Finally, the last principle of money is to give freely—without expecting anything in return. There's joy in giving when you do it from the heart. Giving enables us to make a positive impact on the world.

There are so many ways we can give, such as volunteering our time at a local school or giving money to support those less fortunate. When you give, it has a boomerang effect, because even though you're the one giving, you'll also find yourself on the receiving end.

I enjoy giving with a purpose, especially when I am moved by a reason or need. Giving goes beyond money, time, or things. A simple act of kindness like a smile or a genuine compliment is another form of giving. Sometimes it's the little things that can make the biggest difference in someone's life.

"Too often we underestimate the power of a touch,
a smile, a kind word, a listening ear, an honest compliment,
or the smallest act of caring, all of which have the potential
to turn a life around."
–Leo F. Buscaglia

When I worked at the bank, I heard one of the most touching stories on giving. One morning, our training instructor came in and shared her personal story with us. She started by telling us how thankful she was to have her job. Before working at the bank, she was a single parent struggling to make ends meet, and her life changed for the better after she joined the company.

However, in the beginning, she had a tough time trying to keep up with her bills and expenses. But something amazing and mysterious started to happen. One day, she found an envelope carefully placed on her desk with $20 inside. She was surprised, but she knew the money was for her, so she kept it. Although she was curious about where it came from, she was thankful for the money and put it to good use. Then, the envelopes kept coming every week for a few months straight. As she told the story, you could hear the emotion and sense of gratitude in every word.

That Christmas she decided to hold off on buying a tree until they went on sale later in the season. But one evening, she looked outside her window and found a beautiful Christmas tree with a big bow on top in the backyard. She was so happy to receive such a beautiful tree, but she had no idea where it had come from. And that tree was the last mysterious gift she received. In fact, the envelopes stopped coming that same week. The timing was perfect too, as she was doing much better financially.

Why Give?

Some people struggle with the concept of giving because they are skeptical, often asking questions like: How much of my donation will really end up with the people who need it? Are they really doing anything? Why do they need money anyway?

Sadly, some of them never get past the questions to give anything. For instance, after church one day a friend asked me why I gave money at church. She told me there was no reason to give. I told her that the Bible talks about giving in Malachi.

> *"Will a man rob God? Yet ye have robbed me. But ye say, Wherein have we robbed thee? In tithes and offerings... Bring ye all the tithes into the storehouse, that there may be meat in mine house, and prove me now herewith, saith the LORD of hosts, if I will not open you the windows of heaven, and pour you out a blessing, that there shall not be room enough to receive it."*
> **–Malachi 3:8–10 (King James Version)**

But she was still unconvinced and a bit confused. She just stood there looking at me, waiting for a better reason. So I told her that I gave because I felt it was the right thing to do. And, as you might assume, my simple response was not what she wanted to hear. But it was the truth. As I look back on our conversation, one thing I wish I could have mentioned is that giving opens the door for you to receive more in return. I believe it's a law in life that "what you give comes back tenfold."

The underlying reason many people give is that they have a desire to give, help, and make a difference. For instance, the earthquakes in Haiti and Japan compelled many people to donate money, time, and supplies to help those in need. We are all moved in different ways, and that's the beauty of being who we are individually. Giving has the power to touch people's lives in a positive way and even transform helplessness into hope.

You may believe in giving, or you may be a skeptic like my friend. There are people who think the only way to have financial security is to closely guard and hold on tight to what they have. Such a person is commonly referred to as having "a tight fist" because it would be hard to pry his fingers loose to get him to give. People like this often make excuses such as "I don't have anything to give," "It won't make a difference anyway," or "I don't have the time." Or they simply avoid the subject altogether. If they only knew the power of the words they speak. Remember what I said about mindset? If you say you have nothing to give, then it will be true. Plus, when you have a tight fist, you can't be open to receiving any more than you have, and you may even lose what you thought you had. After all, it is through giving that you open yourself up to receive more in return.

Are You a Giver or a Taker?

"The value of a man resides in what he gives and not in what he is capable of receiving."
—**Albert Einstein**

Are you a giver or a taker? A taker is someone who takes, takes, takes but rarely takes the opportunity to give anything. What's ironic about takers is that they tend to struggle even though they're always receiving things. How can this be?

Is it really better to give than receive? After all, it's been said that when you give it will be abundantly returned back to you. Could that be true? Perhaps that's why billionaires such as Bill Gates and Warren Buffett, who choose to give away millions of dollars to support charities and worthwhile causes, still hold on to their billion-dollar fortunes.

How to Start Giving

You can start giving by first identifying a purpose or cause that you'd like to support. For example, you may want to support a public radio or TV station, nonprofit organization, your alma mater, or some other organization. If your employer has company match programs, be sure to take advantage of them to double the size of your gift.

Keep in mind your support is not limited to monetary donations. You could make food donations to your local food bank, donate gently used items to nonprofit organizations (e.g., Salvation Army, American Red Cross, UNICEF), give blood at the local blood bank, or prepare soldier care packages to send abroad. Whatever the case, here are some tips for giving:

- **Plan ahead.** Use your budget to manage your monetary charitable gifts and donations. For instance, if you tithe 10% of your income, be sure to include it as a line item on your budget.
- **Give what you can afford.** Your donation does not have to be big. Give as much as you can afford. If you don't have the money, consider making nonmonetary (e.g., food, clothing, time) donations instead.
- **Keep your receipts.** Your charitable donations may be tax deductible.
- **Beware of scams.** Yes, there are charitable scams. They may even come to your door asking for a donation. I've found them easier to spot in person, because they always have a specific donation amount they're requesting (e.g., $20) and appear to be uncomfortable answering any specific organization questions. Always check to see if the organization is reputable before donating.

Volunteer Your Time

> *"Life's most persistent and urgent question is,*
> *What are you doing for others?"*
> –Dr. Martin Luther King, Jr.

Life is a journey, and sometimes it feels like we're living it on a speedway. We've become masters of multitasking, yet it still feels as though there are never enough hours in a day. Time is very precious, and the art of prioritization helps us decide how we're going to spend it.

That's why volunteering is another way you can give back. Whether it is volunteering to help build a home, feed the homeless, paint a school, pick up litter, or read to young children, the time you give can make a difference. Plus it makes your own life more meaningful.

For instance, I have spent more than a decade working with Junior Achievement (JA). As its website says, JA "is the world's largest organization dedicated to educating students about workforce readiness, entrepreneurship and financial literacy through experiential, hands-on programs." JA provides a great opportunity to give back to the community and, most importantly, to make a difference in the lives of students.

I encourage you to give your time to make a difference in the lives of others. There are many nonprofit organizations (e.g., Habitat for Humanity, Doctors Without Borders) out there that would welcome your help!

"We make a living by what we get,
but we make a life by what we give."
–Winston Churchill

Key Summary

- Be grateful for what you have today, and you'll have more to appreciate tomorrow.

- Give freely without expecting anything in return. You'll see that giving has a boomerang effect, because even though you're the one giving, you'll find yourself on the receiving end, too.

- Be sure to include your monetary charitable donations in your budget.

- Consider volunteering your time to make a difference in the lives of others.

READY TO TAKE ACTION?

"I did then what I knew how to do.
Now that I know better, I do better."
–Maya Angelou

As this book comes to a close, it brings me great happiness to have shared these personal finance keys to unlock a better financial future with you. This book has revealed the secrets that many people have used to manage money effectively and build wealth. It's true that knowledge is power, but to accomplish anything in life you have to take action.

To *Get Your Money Right*, you must find the courage to take action. Remember you control your own destiny. You have to:
1. Make the decision to change
2. Be committed to succeed

When you make a decision to change and work toward it with unwavering faith, you can accomplish anything! You just have to have the vision and truly believe in yourself. After all, it's your commitment and persistence that breed success.

"You might well remember that nothing can
bring you success but yourself."
–Napoleon Hill

When it comes to personal finance, get personal, because it's your money and no one will ever care more about it than YOU. So use the principles of effective money management to take control of your money yourself!

I encourage you to focus on each key individually, so you have a clearer understanding of the financial principle presented. Spend a week (at minimum) practicing and applying the key in your life. Experts say it takes twenty-one days to form a new habit. Using this learning strategy should help you develop new money habits.

"We are what we repeatedly do,
excellence then is not an act, but a habit."
–Aristotle

To enhance your learning experience further, you may choose to organize a book club in which you discuss the keys and share your experiences and techniques.

I wish you success on your journey. During the times when you might feel discouraged, I suggest you think about those simple yet inspiring words of the little engine in that children's book . . . "I think I can, I think I can." Because I'm convinced if you think you can do it, you will.

"We would accomplish many more things
if we did not think of them as impossible."
– C. Malesherbes

Keep in mind that real change comes from the inside out, so if you think it, say it, and keep working toward it, you're destined for success. And I would love to hear about your successes. Please contact me at kembalaevans.com or write to me at:

Kembala Evans
P.O. Box 59722
Schaumburg, IL 60159-0722

I strongly urge you to continue to build your personal finance knowledge, because the financial industry is constantly changing. I believe the more you know, the more your money will grow.

Share All You Can . . . To "Pay it Forward"

I would have never been able to share this knowledge with you had it not been for the many people who shared theirs with me. So I hope you "pay it forward" too. There are many ways you can share the knowledge. For example, you could participate in a financial literacy group, volunteer with JA, or help your friends and family develop good money management skills. Or you might consider buying a book for someone else to share the knowledge. Once you're well on your way to a better financial future, you may even be inspired to mentor others on their journeys.

Best Wishes,

Kembala Evans

> *"Start where you are, with what you have. Make something of it. Never be satisfied."*
> –**George Washington Carver**

ABOUT THE AUTHOR

Kembala Evans is the founder and president of KP Evans Financial, a personal finance education and coaching firm focused on educating, motivating, and empowering people to take control of their financial futures. She is passionate about helping people transform their lives and achieve success.

Kembala has twelve years of business consulting experience working with *Fortune* 500 clients at Accenture. As an experienced executive, she managed multi-million dollar programs and held a number of positions.

She has a bachelor of business administration in marketing and management from the University of Miami. Kembala lives in the suburbs of Chicago with her husband, Sam, and their two daughters, Aaliyah and Kiara.

Visit KembalaEvans.com for information on speaking, coaching, or to contact the author.

Check out her blog at GainMoneyControl.com or follow her at twitter.com/Kembala.

WHAT IS JUNIOR ACHIEVEMENT?

5% of all author royalties are donated to Junior Achievement.

Junior Achievement (JA) is America's largest and fastest growing non-profit organization dedicated to financial literacy, entrepreneurship, and work readiness skills, with a mission to prepare and inspire young people to succeed in a global economy.

Today, JA realizes its mission through use of a broad spectrum of programs that escalate in sophistication as students progress from kindergarten through 12th grade. In partnership with businesses and educators, JA uses hands-on activities, taught by external volunteers from local businesses and organizations to help young people understand the economics of life.

Through our volunteers and their involvement, JA programs teach young people about the economic realities of life and the importance of staying in school, a decision that plays an important role in a child's success into his/her adult life.

To find your local Junior Achievement office and information on how to get involved, visit www.ja.org and find the "JA Near You" menu. Here you'll find links on opportunities and how to get involved with JA in your town!

CPSIA information can be obtained at www.ICGtesting.com
Printed in the USA
LVOW070342020113

314000LV00002B/6/P